A TIGER AMONG US

A TIGER AMONG US

A STORY OF VALOR IN VIETNAM'S A SHAU VALLEY

BENNIE G. ADKINS, CSM (US ARMY, RET.)
AND KATIE LAMAR JACKSON

FOREWORD BY CHUCK HAGEL

DA CAPO PRESS

Da Capo Press
Hachette Book Group
1290 Avenue of the Americas, New York, NY 10104
www.dacapopress.com
@DaCapoPress

Printed in the United States of America

First Edition: May 2018

Published by Da Capo Press, an imprint of Perseus Books, LLC,
a subsidiary of Hachette Book Group, Inc.
The Da Capo Press name and logo is a trademark of The Hachette Book Group.

The publisher is not responsible for websites (or their content) that are not owned by the publisher.

Cataloging-in-Publication data for this book is available from the Library of Congress.

Editorial production by Christine Marra, *Marra*thon Production Services.
www.marrathoneditorial.org

Print book interior design by Jane Raese.
Set in 13-point Granjon

Cataloging-in-Publication data for this book is available from the Library of Congress.
ISBN 978-0-306-90202-4 (hardcover)
ISBN 978-0-306-90204-8 (ebook)

LSC-C
10 9 8 7 6 5 4 3 2 1

TO ALL SEVENTEEN
SPECIAL FORCES SOLDIERS
WHO FOUGHT IN
THE BATTLE OF A SHAU

CONTENTS

FOREWORD

It's important to tell stories about bravery and valor in the face of battle, but it is equally important to tell stories about resilience in life—a soldier's story before and, if they are lucky enough to survive a conflict, after a battle. It's those stories that paint a picture of the courage and resourcefulness it takes to live through a battle and then go on to a life well lived. The complete picture.

Bennie G. Adkins's story exemplifies that very thing. When he left the rural Oklahoma farm of his childhood to join the army, he didn't set out to become a hero. He just saw more opportunity in the military than on the farm. And when, out of boredom, he volunteered for the special forces and made it through the grueling training required to wear a green beret, he didn't plan to find himself in a remote valley in Vietnam fighting a grueling thirty-eight-hour battle for his life and the lives of others. He was to serve three nonconsecutive tours in Vietnam. He was sent back to Vietnam to carry out the stealthy, hush-hush work of Studies and Observation Group maneuvers; he didn't plan on being so effective at his job that the enemy put a price on his head. But he did all of those things.

But after his tours in Vietnam, his story continued. Adkins returned stateside to spend another seven years in the military, reaching the rank of command sergeant major before retiring to start a new life as a successful businessman and teacher. Sergeant majors are a force unto themselves. I used to say that generals are important but sergeants major are essential—and they scare the hell out of me! Bennie probably didn't know that it would take bravery and toughness to make that new life for himself and his family during a time when Vietnam veterans were far from respected. But he did just that for another twenty-two years, during which time he and his wife, Mary, fearlessly moved on with life.

Though he was nominated for the Medal of Honor just after the 1966 battle in which he fought so tirelessly and valiantly, and he was awarded a host of other military honors for his exemplary service during his military career, the true measure of his valor was not fully recognized until almost fifty years later. Thanks to the hard work and tenacity of a number of his military peers who believed in Adkins's worth and his heroic actions, in 2014 he finally stood on a stage at the White House as the Medal of Honor was placed around his neck by the president of the United States.

Adkins will tell you that he wears that medal proudly today, not for himself, though his actions in that battle and beyond are legendary, but for the sixteen other men who fought with him in that horrendous battle. I say he also wears it to show that battles are fought on many fronts, and in doing so he illustrates that being brave and resilient in life is truly a soldier's story.

It's a story worth reading and a life worth remembering. For all of us in life, regardless of our station, circumstances, or position, our most important responsibility is to be a good role model for others to follow. Parents especially are charged with this responsibility. Bennie Adkins has been an exceptional role model to all in every phase of his life. The highest compliment.

—Chuck Hagel
Former Secretary of Defense and
Senator from Nebraska
February 2018

PREFACE

It's been more than fifty years since sixteen other Green Berets and I fought at the 1966 Battle of A Shau, and a lot of things, good and bad, have happened in my life since then.

That battle and other events that occurred during my three tours of duty in Vietnam (from 1963 to 1971) are certainly experiences I will never forget, but until 2014 I had pretty much put them behind me and moved on with my life.

Then, on June 11, 2014, I got a phone call from US President Barack Obama saying he had approved the awarding of a Medal of Honor to me in recognition of my activities at A Shau nearly five decades before.

That phone call changed my life. I went from being an eighty-year-old semi-retired businessman in Opelika, Alabama, to a member of a small but elite group of Americans who have been chosen to wear the Medal of Honor, the nation's highest medal for valor in combat that can be awarded to members of the armed forces.

As of the writing of this book, only about thirty-five hundred Americans have been awarded the Medal of Honor since it was first established in 1861, and only seventy-two of us are alive today to wear it.

The Medal of Honor is awarded by the president of the United States in the name of the US Congress, and there are three versions of it: one for the army, another for the navy, and a third for the air force. I wear the army Medal of Honor, which consists of a gold five-pointed star, each ray of which is tipped with a green oak leaf, and all of them are interlaced with a wreath of green and gold. In the middle of the star is the profile of the Roman goddess of war, Minerva, wearing a battle helmet, and she is surrounded by the words UNITED STATES OF AMERICA. Attached above the star is a gold bar inscribed with the word VALOR, and on top of that is an eagle with its wings spread wide.

The medal hangs from a light-blue silk ribbon connected to a shield of the same color decorated with thirteen white stars representing the thirteen original colonies. Those same thirteen stars are also emblazoned on the Medal of Honor flag, which has been presented to Medal of Honor recipients since 2001.

I received the Medal of Honor on September 15, 2014, during a ceremony at the White House, and I received the Medal of Honor flag the following day when I was inducted into the Pentagon's Hall of Heroes. I was humbled to receive both.

When I wear the medal out in public, many people either recognize it or stop and ask about it, so I have a chance to explain what it is, how I came to wear it, and why I am so proud to wear it.

Here's what I say every chance I get:

"I was awarded the Medal of Honor for my actions during a battle in the Vietnam War, but I *wear* it in honor of others. I wear it for the more than fifty million men and women who have served our country in both times of war and peace.

I wear it to remind us all of their sacrifices and how so few of them have worked so hard to keep so many of us safe throughout our nation's history. [Today, our military represents just one percent of our nation's entire population.] I also wear it to honor the 2.7 million Americans who fought in Vietnam, especially the more than fifty-eight thousand who died there, twelve hundred of which never came home."

But most important of all, I tell them that I am honored and humbled to wear the Medal of Honor not for myself, but for the sixteen other men who fought with me during the Battle of A Shau in March 1966, five of whom paid the ultimate price.

This book tells the story of that battle and of my experiences before, during, and after the fighting there, so it is told from my point of view. But I realize there were things I might not remember or things that happened to me that were different from what happened to the sixteen other US Special Forces soldiers who fought with me.

Because I wanted this book to be as accurate and truthful as possible, my co-author and I worked hard to gather stories from the other men who were there. By the time we started this book in 2015, I knew of only six A Shau veterans who were still alive—myself, Davis Blair, Victor Underwood, John Bradford, Wayne Murray, and George Pointon. Since that time one of those brave men, Wayne Murray, has passed away, but we were lucky that all five of these men were willing to share their stories with us, and let us offer at least a glimpse of those stories in this book's pages. We have also been lucky to have access to old records and after-action reports, most of which were provided to us by Vic Underwood and Dave Blair.

I also wanted this book to properly reflect on the US Army Special Forces. For those readers unfamiliar with the Special Forces, here's a little background.

The very first official US Army Special Forces unit, 10th Special Forces Group (Airborne), was formed in June 1952 and given the primary mission of training, equipping, advising, and assisting foreign forces. Prior to that, Special Forces soldiers from the United States and other countries had honed their skills while working in Eastern Europe, the Philippines, and a number of other theaters of war and conflict across the world. Through the years, US Special Forces soldiers have operated in places such as Vietnam, El Salvador, Panama, Haiti, Somalia, Bosnia, Kosovo, the Middle East, the Philippines, and Africa, to name a few. Their experiences laid the foundation for our modern Special Forces program.

Today, there are some nine thousand Special Forces troops who serve in one of five active-duty and two National Guard groups. As they did in my day, these Special Forces units are designed around a twelve-man team of two commanding officers and ten enlisted men. Two of those enlisted men are experts in weapons, two in engineering, two in communications, two in operations and intelligence, and two in medicine. Because two men on each team have shared expertise, this means a Special Forces team can be split into two groups of six with each group retaining the full complement of skills and knowledge, allowing for a multiplier effect.

Exceptional training and this unique division of skills have been the trademarks of Special Forces soldiers for more than sixty years, and it is that training and our ability to work as a team that, I believe, kept me alive to be able to humbly wear the Medal of Honor.

I'll tell more about how Special Forces works and my experience as a Special Forces soldier in this book, and also more about my experience in the Battle of A Shau and in life, but while the story in this book focuses on my life and my experiences, it, like the Medal of Honor I wear, does not belong to me and me alone. It belongs to the sixteen Special Forces soldiers who fought with me at A Shau. It also belongs to the other people who have stood beside me all of these years, my family.

I hope we have done them all justice.

Bennie G. Adkins, csm (US Army, Ret.),
Medal of Honor recipient

PREY

N O LONGER TRAPPED LIKE ANIMALS in our small, dilapidated Special Forces training camp, we were now being hunted like animals in the jungle of Vietnam's A Shau Valley.

Of the seventeen Special Forces soldiers stationed at Camp A Shau in the early spring of 1966, only thirteen of us were still alive, and only eleven of us—all badly wounded from thirty-eight hours of battling a force of North Vietnamese soldiers that outnumbered us ten to one—were still on the ground and fighting.

We knew the battle was unwinnable, but we were Green Berets. We didn't give up. And not a one of us intended to be taken prisoner. We'd made up our minds about that in the early hours of the battle, and we each had our own plan to make sure we were not taken alive. My plan was to take a North Vietnamese Army (NVA) officer prisoner and hold him hostage while I escaped into Laos.

We were, however, doing everything we could to stay alive and defend our camp, so when the call came in late on the afternoon of March 10, 1966, from our higher-ups to abandon the camp, we reluctantly followed orders.

Following those orders, however, was not as easy as walking out of the camp and getting on one of the US Marine helicopters sent in to evacuate us. The enemy was all over our camp. We were completely overrun. We were fighting them off almost hand to hand, fighting through a wall of them to get to the helicopters.

When I finally made it out of the camp, the evacuation landing zone was an absolute fiasco. A large number of the South Vietnamese special forces troops—our friendlies—had decided they had priority to get on the helicopters before anyone else, and they were mobbing the helicopters and shooting each other. The NVA was also shooting at us. It was a horrible mess.

At that time I was with a small group of two Americans, one of whom was mortally wounded and on a stretcher, and five or six Chinese Nung (a Vietnamese ethnic group). I knew we couldn't make it if we went toward the fighting, so I made the decision to head into the jungle north of the camp toward higher ground, and away from the action.

Our group made it away undetected, but shortly after that our fatally wounded fellow American died, and all I could do was cache his body, then keep moving. The NVA didn't know to look for us—they were busy fighting the rest of what was left of our troops—so we were able to make our way without much trouble for a while, moving toward the northwest where we hoped to get across the Vietnam-Laos border.

We spent that first night in the jungle lying low in the dark, but the next morning we were moving again, and we knew there were support people flying overhead. I managed to use a little FM radio I had brought with me out of the camp to communicate with a nearby fixed-wing aircraft, and they sent in two helicopters to get us.

For a landing zone, we picked a fairly open area with small trees and cut the trees, pushing them over on each other to make a landing pad just big enough for one helicopter to come in at a time. As the first helicopter came down, though, some of the NVA—they must have heard the helicopter and come to see what was happening—shot it down on the pad.

Two of the helicopter's four-member Marine crew were injured in the crash, so the second helicopter, which couldn't land, dropped ropes. We hooked the two wounded crewmen onto the ropes and they were lifted out. But that's all the second helicopter could handle, so with two of the remaining Marine crew members now in our ranks, we were left on the ground to fend for ourselves.

By this time it was getting late and the weather, so foggy it seemed like we were in a constant drizzle, was getting worse. We knew there was no chance another helicopter could come in for us that afternoon, so our only choice was to keep moving.

We continued pushing our way through the jungle, stopping every three or four hours to exchange fire with the NVA, who were now following us, then moving on again. As night came and ended our second day in the jungle, we found a little area on high ground and decided that was where we would spend the night.

That night as we sat still and quiet, I could hear the usual bugs and monkeys of the jungle. I could also hear the North Vietnamese soldiers talking to one another all around us. They were close, but they couldn't seem to find us.

We thought we were secure for the moment until I noticed another noise. Something was moving through the brush. Something large.

I began to hear a little growl or two and then I saw it—a pair of yellow eyes reflecting the little light that filtered through the jungle's darkness. That's when I realized we were now the prey of not just the NVA, but also of a four-hundred-pound Indochinese tiger drawn to us by the smell of our blood and crud.

CHAPTER ONE

DE OPPRESSO LIBER AND THE ART OF BEING UNCONVENTIONAL

W**E'VE GOT A LOT OF NICKNAMES**—"Quiet Professionals," "Soldier-Diplomats," "Snake-eaters," "Sneaky Petes," "Green Beanies"— and a lot of different words have been used to describe us: *rogue, independent, arrogant, undisciplined, renegade, prima donnas, crazy.*

Maybe we are all of those things at times and, yes, you do have to be a little crazy to be a Green Beret. But in my view, the word that best describes us is *unconventional.*

That's because everything about us is unconventional. The way we dress, the way we wear our hair, the weapons we use, the things we eat, the way we train, and even the way we think are often unorthodox. I guess we didn't seem like a highly disciplined military unit, which may be one reason the regular army folks didn't appreciate us, but that's not so. Green Berets were, and still are, highly disciplined and highly trained.

We had to be in order to do our jobs—jobs that included things like reconnaissance, direct action, counterterrorism, hostage rescue, humanitarian and peacekeeping assistance, and our trademark job, conducting and providing training to foreign forces in the use of unconventional warfare.

To do all of those jobs, we had to know how to fight, but we also had to know how to get in and out of places and situations undetected, not a shot fired. And we had to know how to build relationships with people of all cultures and nations.

Most of all, we had to believe that, whatever the job, we had each other's backs. And we had to be committed to our motto, *De oppresso liber,* "To free the oppressed."

But I didn't know any of that back in 1961 when I signed up to become a member of the US Army Special Forces. I was just bored.

MY NAME IS BENNIE GENE ADKINS and this is the story of how I, a conventional Oklahoma farm boy more accustomed to picking cotton than picking up a gun, became a Green Beret. It's also the story of how, as a member of America's elite unconventional warfare team, I ended up in a remote South Vietnamese jungle being stalked by North Vietnamese soldiers and a hungry tiger.

My story begins in Waurika, Oklahoma, on February 1, 1934, when I was born into a large and loving family of six boys and one girl. I was right in the middle of the litter, and we lived out in the country in a one-story house that had four bedrooms, and, for most of my growing-up years, no inside bathroom.

A lot of people would say we were super poor, but we didn't realize it. We always had an abundance of food because we had a garden and we kept hogs, chickens, and even a few sheep sometimes. And we always had eight or ten Jersey cows that we hand-milked twice a day, every day, so we had plenty of milk to drink and sell. We also grew corn, small grains, and hay to feed the cows, and cotton was our primary cash crop, the short-staple kind that you harvest by picking the whole burr off the plant, not just the boll.

My brothers, sister, and I grew up picking that cotton, milking those cows, and doing whatever else was needed to keep the farm going day to day, year to year. We and our parents were the primary farm labor, so we all had to get up early in the morning and do chores before the school bus came, and it came early because we lived almost eight miles outside of town at the back end of the bus route.

I liked school okay and I excelled a little there. I took a lot of agriculture electives and served as president of our school's Future Farmers of America club for three years, and was president of my freshman, sophomore, and junior classes, too. I also played some sports—football, basketball, baseball, and boxing—but those took too much time away from my farm chores, which I had to do in the afternoons as well as in the mornings.

There's a story that goes with that, though. My mother decided I had probably worked enough with the boxing—she was worried I might get hurt, I think—and told me I was not to box anymore. But being about fifteen or sixteen years old, I entered a local tournament anyway. As it would happen, I won the tournament and my picture appeared on the front page of the paper. You might have guessed it, that put an end to my boxing career. And after that I didn't pursue any sports real heavily, though there came a time a few years later when some of my sports experience was pretty useful to me.

When I got ready to graduate from Waurika High School in 1952, I was thinking I'd go into agriculture. It's what I knew the most about. But I also knew that finding land was tough. Our family farmed more than three hundred acres, all of it rented, and at the time some big, rich ranchers were purchasing all the farmland at a higher price than I could have afforded. Farming did not look promising to me, and I decided I wanted a different life, a better life, so I elected to attempt some college life.

I first went over to Southeastern State Teachers College in Durant, Oklahoma, more than one hundred miles from Waurika, and I fared okay there—not great, but okay. But it was too far from my family, so I changed to Cameron Junior College in Lawton, Oklahoma, just about sixty miles from home.

I guess I wasn't really ready for college. My high school had not prepared me well for college classes, since we didn't have chemistry and other college-prep courses, and, to be honest, I was more interested in the pretty girls than in my schoolbooks. The bottom line is, I didn't do too well academically and my dad decided maybe he was wasting his money on me in college, so I dropped out and began working at any odd jobs I could find—as a fry cook in some of the fast-food places and that type of work, about all that was available for young people in the Waurika area at that time.

Of course, by dropping out of school, that moved me to the top of the draft list, but when my draft number came up it didn't bother me too much because it was peacetime and, thinking about my other choices of being a fry cook or a farmer, the military looked like a pretty good opportunity. So when, on December 5, 1956, I was inducted into the US Army and sent to basic training at Fort Bliss, Texas, I was not unhappy about the situation.

I was a green recruit and it showed, especially compared to some of the others in my basic training group who were coming back into the service and had more experience. But I did do well with the physical part of basic training. I guess the sports I'd played in school and the hard work on the farm helped me with that.

After basic training, I did my military occupational specialty (MOS) training to become an administrative clerk-typist, and then the military decided to send me overseas where I was assigned to a US Army Europe (USAREUR) subpost in Giessen, Germany. Arriving there as a young private, I got a security clearance and went to work in the security and plans section (S2/S3) of the subpost, where I stayed until near the end of my first two years of enlistment.

Giessen was a quiet post, not much action, except I did get to meet Elvis Presley when I was there. I actually fingerprinted him. To be honest, I was not really a fan of Elvis's music, but I always respected him because he served his country. More than Elvis, though, I got to know his father who had come to

Germany to spend time with Elvis and who liked to go down to the commissary and sit around. He might have enjoyed a chew of tobacco while he was there, too.

I did well enough when I was there to be promoted early to sergeant, which in peacetime was super fortunate, and since I'd been promoted I decided to reenlist for a six-year period. I also decided I wanted to become more involved in operations work, so I requested a transfer and was sent to the 2nd Division of the 9th Infantry at Fort Benning, Georgia. This was a basic training unit and I worked in the battalion's S2 (intelligence) section for a while, then changed to a combat support company and worked with the basic trainees on an infiltration range.

On that range, the trainees had to crawl under wire and get some experience with having live ammunition fired over their heads. This was fired high over their heads and the machine gun was braced so it couldn't fire lower, but they didn't know that. My job was to operate that course, which I crawled three or four times a day with the trainees to be sure the explosives were set the way they needed to be.

After a period of time, though, this was boring to me, and I knew it was not what I really wanted to do. I had heard about an organization called the Army Special Forces and that sounded more interesting. Looking back on it, if I had really known what I was getting into I might not have volunteered, but once I got started I had too much pride to quit. And I can tell you that, without Special Forces, I would not have made a military career.

That's because at the time in most of the military, commissioned officers looked down on enlisted men, even if they were as well trained and capable as the officers themselves. By this time, I had figured out that I was not suited to work for someone who might be less competent than I was, but Special Forces was not that way. In Special Forces if you weren't competent you didn't last long, and you were respected as an individual for what you could do, not for your rank.

It wasn't easy to become a Special Forces soldier. I was tested mentally and physically, and it was such a difficult program that even today only about 3 percent of the people who apply make it through. What made it even harder in my time was that the selection process they used to evaluate us was not done by a committee; it was done by the older, more experienced Special Forces people who were going out and training with us recruits. They worked with us on a daily basis and they knew what we could or couldn't do.

To join Special Forces you had to be a triple volunteer: you had to volunteer for the regular army, you had to volunteer to be a paratrooper, and you had to volunteer for Special Forces.

Of course, I had already "volunteered" for the army thanks to the draft, and I had volunteered for and completed Airborne School at Benning, where I was fortunate to come out of jump school ranked number three in a class of fifty or sixty soldiers. To me, parachuting was just a way of getting to the battle, just like some people commute a long way to work.

So I volunteered a third time to join the Army Special Forces in 1961, and was soon accepted into what is now known as the Special Forces Qualification Course (or informally the "Q Course," but during my time it was all so new it didn't have an official name) at Fort Bragg, North Carolina. It was there I began to learn the individual and team skills that set Special Forces soldiers apart from other branches of the military.

My class members and I started every morning in garrison with thirty to forty minutes of calisthenics—the Daily Dozen of push-ups, squats, toe touches, jumping jacks, lunges, leg lifts, and the like. Then we would go for a four-mile run (some of the men liked to think they could do a little better and would occasionally go five or six miles) in formation and in combat boots. We'd try to make the four miles in thirty-two minutes, about an eight-minute mile, which was moving along at a pretty good clip.

After that we would shower and dress for the day's training, which might happen in a classroom where we learned about things like military history and tactics, psychological and guerilla warfare, planning, logistics, foreign languages and cultures, and that sort of thing. Or we might be outside refreshing our skills or learning new ones, such as the use of various weapons and explosives (including atomic weapons), map and compass reading, and marksmanship.

As the training progressed, we learned about small-unit tactics and survival, evasion, resistance, and escape (SERE) techniques such as wilderness survival, firecraft, food and water procurement and purification, mountaineering, rappelling, and the like. There were lots of training sessions in the dark, too, including nighttime parachute jumps and infiltration maneuvers.

After we completed that initial general training, which took about three months, we began our MOS training in one of five specialties: weapons, engineering, medical, operations and intelligence (O&I), and communications. We spent the next nine months or so undergoing intensive training, a lot of that training coming from veteran Green Berets who had experience they passed along to us.

The training, of course, varied depending on the MOS.

Of all the MOS positions, the medical sergeants were probably the most important and highly skilled individuals on a team. They had to be super intelligent because they trained to be the equivalent of a physician's assistant, but one who could do anything from treating traumatic battle wounds to delivering babies to pulling rotten teeth.

Weapons sergeants were taught to assemble and disassemble every small-arms weapon in the world, and they learned to fire and usually qualified with those weapons, too. This had become a necessity at that time, because none of us ever knew what country we would be in, or what kinds of weapons we might end up using.

The engineers learned how to build things and how to blow them up. When they were in the field they might build a school or dig a well one day, then go out and utilize mines and booby traps the next. They learned how to improvise, too, to the point that they could go into an everyday kitchen and find enough supplies to make an explosive.

Communications sergeants had to know how to use AM and FM radios, send and receive International Morse Code, and even how to make their own antennas, to the point that they could come into a room and plug into the electrical system and use it for an antenna.

O&I specialists, my MOS, had to learn to use both conventional and unconventional warfare tactics and techniques to collect and process intelligence for special missions and operations. We were also taught how to interrogate prisoners, establish and provide security for a camp or operation, maintain classified documents in the operational area, and establish and carry out destruction and evacuation plans. We trained on how to write an operation order, but also how to prepare troops and the information necessary for the development of an operation, such as reconnaissance and training, and how to rehearse for it.

The intelligence training was focused on the methods of obtaining information through operations, or through interrogation of prisoners and local civilians or local agents who might be supplying you with information, either voluntarily or for pay.

Though each of us had a specialty, every one of us also had to cross-train in those specialties, the real strength of Special Forces. We all knew enough about each other's jobs that we could take up the slack if one of us was out of commission.

As we perfected our skills, we could also volunteer to qualify in other specialty areas such as sniper, scuba, and high-altitude, low-opening (HALO) training. I "volunteered," which in Special Forces was something like "You go over there and do it," and qualified in all three of those specialties.

HALO parachuting was fairly new at that time, and in training it required you to jump out of an airplane at a high altitude (up to thirty-five thousand feet), do a free fall for a period of time, and open your chute at a much lower level, as low as two thousand feet. This is especially good for not being detected in the air, and it lets you track (position your body for accelerated forward speed and to move away from other jumpers) to the location you need to go, but it takes a great deal of training to master the skill.

You do fall a long way fast with a HALO jump, often about three miles in two and a half minutes, but the falling is not as hard as the tracking. The other problem is with your eyes, because if you aren't careful and don't have your goggles locked on good, you'll lose them. If you lose your goggles and you're falling with your eyes open, it can eventually cause damage to the eyes. Despite all of this, I liked doing HALO jumps and did them a number of times during my years in Special Forces.

Keep in mind that in Special Forces we used our MOS skills for a variety of purposes, not all of which were about warfare. Many people don't realize that Green Berets are, first and foremost, teachers. We train people at every level, from a head of government to the squad and individual soldier level to civilians in a community.

A good example is that in Vietnam, Special Forces medics and engineers helped train people in villages to become soldiers, but they also taught them how to keep their families safe by showing them how to build wells, keep their water supply clean, and even how to take care of themselves with good hygiene by teaching them things like how to make soap. I can tell you that if you take a gallon of pork skins, a can of lye, and a gallon of water and boil it all until the pork skins dissolve, you can dry it down into a rough lye soap that will clean anything, including the skin off your hands.

So our Special Forces training, which usually lasted about two and a half years, had many uses, and it took us through many levels, including a final test when we were sent out into the field on a mock mission to practice all we had learned. This exercise is now called "Robin Sage," but when I was going through it didn't have a name. It was just a field training exercise where we went out into the woods for about a month and were expected to run our missions and survive. For this exercise, we were sent into the wilds of North Carolina (they call the area "Pineland" nowadays).

I remember when I went it was wintertime and we had mock "aggressors" after us. As part of our mission, we had to blow up a bridge that the aggressor force was going to use, and the only way we could figure out to get to the bridge, which was being guarded by the aggressors, was to get in the water. We drew straws for that duty and I lost. You talk about cold; that was cold.

If you managed to finish the program and graduate, though, you finally got to wear the beret, that unconventional hat that sets us apart from all other sections of the military. You were also ready to go into action.

I was awarded my beret in late 1962, and I remember this because about that time they pulled me out to go to the Bay of Pigs. The United States was there to support rebels who wanted to overthrow the Cuban government, and I found myself sitting in a submarine off the coast of Cuba waiting on the decision about whether we would go ashore. This decision became negative and we did not deploy, which was not completely unheard of with Special Forces. There were a number of times when I was trained and ready for deployment and my mission was aborted or changed at the last minute.

I don't recall attending a graduation ceremony when I officially got my Special Forces tab and my green beret. What I do remember, though, was another big ceremony that happened the year before.

That ceremony occurred on October 12, 1961, while I was still in the qualification phase of the program, and President John F. Kennedy came to Fort Bragg to tour the fort and the US Army Special Warfare Center, home of Army Special Forces. It was Kennedy who had reinvigorated the Special Forces, which was initially founded in 1952 but had been cut back in the intervening years. Soon after he was sworn in as president in January 1961, Kennedy deployed several hundred Special Forces soldiers to South Vietnam to be special advisors in the fight against the North Vietnamese and the Viet Cong. He believed in what the Special Forces could do for our country early on, and seeing us in action made him even more of a believer.

While he was visiting Fort Bragg that day, Kennedy was told by our camp's commander, Brigadier General William Yarborough, that Special Forces soldiers wanted to wear green berets, which they had worn informally from 1954 to 1956 until they were banned because they looked too "foreign," as a sign of their unique role in the US military.

After watching the Special Forces soldiers perform demonstrations at the camp that day, Kennedy sent a message to Yarborough stating: "The challenge of this old but new form of operations is a real one and I know that you and the members of your Command will carry on for us and the free world in a manner which is both worthy and inspiring. I am sure that the Green Beret will be a mark of distinction in the trying times ahead."

Shortly after that, Kennedy officially authorized us to wear the green beret as a mark of distinction, which it remains today, and which I proudly wore throughout my years in Special Forces.

From that time on, Kennedy was a favorite of the Green Berets, and when he was killed in November 1963, we all felt like we had lost a true ally in Washington. We wanted to show our respect for him and at some point before the funeral, I was volunteered to be one of the Special Forces men making a parachute jump into Arlington National Cemetery as part of his funeral service. I recall we did several training jumps to prepare for that event and at the last minute it was cancelled. But that's how it was in Special Forces. You never knew what would happen from one day to the next.

CHAPTER TWO

GREEN BERETS AT WORK

O**NCE I WAS AN OFFICIAL** Green Beret, I couldn't tell much difference in my life. That's probably because very little changed in my day-to-day life from being a trainee to becoming Special Forces qualified.

We did get a little more money in our per diem payments when we were on temporary duty (TDY), but otherwise I still got up every morning and went to work and kept training and cross-training intensely.

Fort Bragg was then, and still is, the command center for US Special Forces, and the work of all Special Forces groups, located across the United States, is led from there. At that time Fort Bragg was also home to my group, the 5th Special Forces Group, now based at Fort Campbell, Kentucky. All the groups were realigned in the early 2000s, and there are now five active duty and two Army National Guard Special Forces groups.

Today, these include 1st Special Forces Group, headquartered at Joint Base Lewis-McChord, Washington, oriented toward the Pacific region of the world; 3rd Special Forces Group, headquartered at Fort Bragg, North Carolina, oriented toward most of Sub-Saharan Africa; 5th Special Forces Group at Fort Campbell, oriented toward the Middle East, Persian Gulf, Central Asia, and the Horn of Africa; 7th Special Forces Group, headquartered at Eglin Air Force Base, Florida, and oriented toward the western hemisphere (South and Central America and the Caribbean); 10th Special Forces Group, headquartered at Fort Carson, Colorado, oriented toward Europe and parts of Turkey, Israel, Lebanon, and North Africa; 19th Special Forces Group, a National Guard Special Forces group headquartered in Draper, Utah, and oriented toward Southwest Asia, Europe, and Southeast Asia; and 20th Special Forces Group, another National Guard group headquartered in Birmingham, Alabama, that covers parts of Latin America, the Caribbean, the Gulf of Mexico, and the southwestern Atlantic Ocean.

Because each Special Forces group has a specific regional focus, soldiers assigned to these groups concentrate on learning the tactics, languages, and cultures of those specific regions, though they may be deployed outside of their areas of operation when they are needed elsewhere.

Within those groups are battalions, and in each battalion there are three companies—Alpha, Bravo, and Charlie—which are also known by their operational detachment designations (ODs) and which usually go by the names C Team (ODC), B Team (ODB), and A Team (ODA).

The C Team serves as the headquarters element of the battalion, while the B Team serves as the headquarters element for the company and provides support, both in garrison and in the field, for the A Team. The A Team typically conducts direct operations; however, B Teams are sometimes deployed into hostile areas as extra backup for the A Teams.

A Teams are set up to have twelve members—a detachment commander and an assistant detachment commander, both of whom are usually commissioned officers, and ten enlisted men. Those ten men include an operations sergeant (also known as a team sergeant, who is in charge of O&I work), a master sergeant (who serves as the assistant operations sergeant), two weapons sergeants, two engineering sergeants, two medical sergeants, and two communications sergeants.

By having two people qualified as specialists in each of those categories, a twelve-member team has the ability to do "split team" operations—they can divide into two six-member teams and still have all the specialties covered, which serves as a force multiplier.

Once I qualified for Special Forces and became an A Team member, I was available for deployment at any time, such as my first mission to Cuba back in April 1961 when I was sitting at ready on that submarine. I never knew from day to day where I might be sent, and sometimes I would be tapped for short missions focused on specific operations, like the Bay of Pigs, or chosen for longer missions, which during my time in Special Forces included deployments to Vietnam, Laos, Cambodia, and other places.

At the time, Special Forces was not necessarily under the authority of the ground commanders in a foreign country. Instead, while in theater, our units might report directly to US Special Operations Command (USSOCOM, or SOCOM) or other command authorities, or we might be working for the Central Intelligence Agency (CIA) or other similar organizations.

Though we were not officially at war in Vietnam in 1963, the United States had been heavily involved in training South Vietnamese troops beginning in 1954, when an American Military Assistance and Advisory Group (MAAG) had been established there. Through MAAG, US Special Forces soldiers were the primary trainers and advisors for the Army of the Republic of South Vietnam (ARVN) against the North Vietnamese Army. But we also were advising a lot of other groups, such as the Civilian Irregular Defense Group (CIDG) forces, local citizens, and other US military units. As a Special Forces soldier there, you could be advising anyone from a raw recruit all the way up to a head of government.

I left for my first deployment to the Republic of Vietnam in February 1963, arriving there in civilian clothes. I didn't really know who was paying me or who my bosses were, but it didn't matter. I was there to do a job and I absolutely believed in what I was doing. I wanted to defend my country and I believed in our motto, *De oppresso liber*—"To free the oppressed."

CHAPTER THREE

A FIRST LOOK

W HEN I ARRIVED IN VIETNAM in 1963 as a young sergeant, I was assigned as a replacement on a Special Forces team that had just laid out a camp in Gia Vuc, a village that straddled a major infiltration route in this extremely mountainous, sparsely populated region of Vietnam.

Camp Gia Vuc, located about eighty miles from Da Nang and about fifty miles from Quang Ngai City, a large city on the East Sea, was an old French camp that had been reopened in early 1962 as a Civilian Irregular Defense Group (CIDG) camp.

CIDG camps were set up by the US government during the Vietnam War to develop South Vietnamese military units from Vietnam's various minority populations. The CIDG program was first set up in 1961 by the CIA as a way to overcome the Viet Cong's influence and growth in the Central Highlands area of South Vietnam. From the get-go, they used Special Forces soldiers to train villagers on how to protect themselves and to become soldiers for the South Vietnamese military.

By the time I got there in 1963, control of the camps had been turned over to the South Vietnamese special forces, the Luc Luong Dac Biet (LLDB), and we were there primarily as trainers, though we also provided security, intelligence, and interdiction services. (As the US presence in South Vietnam grew, so did the number of these camps, and at one time during the war there were better than sixty of them in operation.)

When I was there, Camp Gia Vuc was small (though I think it developed later into a larger camp). It was just a few hundred feet long and, like most of the CIDG camps at that time, was close to a Montagnard village.

Montagnards are an indigenous minority group of people who once lived isolated, primitive lives in Vietnam's mountain regions. Much like American Indians here in the United States, they were divided into different tribes. There were as many as thirty such tribes when I got to Vietnam, each with its own culture and language. These people, also known as "Degas" and "Degars," had been named *Montagnards* by the French when they were fighting in Vietnam, a name that means something like "people of the mountain" or "mountaineers." We also called them "Yards," which we Special Forces guys used as a term of fondness.

Montagnards have been oppressed and discriminated against for centuries by other groups, beginning with the early ethnic Vietnamese (Kinh), who migrated into South Vietnam and pushed these native people away from the coastal areas that had been their original homes and into the mountains.

Through the years after that, French, North Vietnamese, and the Viet Cong occupiers kept infringing on the Montagnards' lands and also made them pawns in their conflicts. Despite all of that, the Montagnards had held on to their own culture because they lived in relative isolation in the Central Highlands.

Most Montagnards worked in slash-and-burn agriculture where they would go into the mountain areas and develop rice fields, orchards, and vegetable gardens, then, once the soil became depleted, would move on to another area and do the same thing all over again.

They looked different from the ethnic, mainstream Vietnamese people. They were about the same size bodywise, but they had darker skin and different eyes, more Polynesian than Asian. They all had long hair, and the women filed their front teeth down, usually into points; their teeth and gums were stained from chewing on betel palm nut, a mild narcotic the women in particular liked to use. It was a good painkiller, but also addictive, and they chewed it like some people do tobacco, its juice turning their mouths, gums, and lips a dark purple color.

They dressed quite differently from other Vietnamese nationals, too. The women were usually topless and wore skirts. The men were shirtless, preferring loincloths over trousers, and couldn't understand why you'd want a shirt.

Though Montagnards might have been primitive, they were important to both sides in the Vietnam War. The Communist North Vietnamese wanted to control the Montagnards, many of whom had been converted to Christianity by French and American missionaries, because they were afraid these people would side with South Vietnam. The South Vietnamese wanted to control them because they were afraid the Montagnards would join the Viet Cong. Add to this that the Montagnards' villages were of strategic value to both sides and the fact that they were excellent warriors, and you'll understand why we all wanted to make inroads with them.

When I got to Vietnam and began teaching Montagnards and other indigenous troops, I quickly learned a lot about South Vietnamese politics and culture, and about the attitudes different groups of Vietnamese had about the growing war and about each other.

One thing I learned was that the Montagnards were an oppressed people, discriminated against by their own countrymen. The ethnic, mainstream South Vietnamese did not like them at all and called them *mi* or *moi*, a derogatory term that meant "savages."

By our cultural standards, I guess they were savages, and they were not well educated, but they were highly intelligent and were super good trackers who could follow a trail almost anywhere. For that reason, and maybe because they were as unconventional as we were, Special Forces soldiers had a great respect for them. And most of them came to respect us, too, fighting and dying with us throughout the war.

Understanding their culture could be a problem sometimes, though, which I learned the hard way when I was at Gia Vuc.

We needed some timbers to build a bunker and we wanted to do everything correctly, so we went to the village chief and asked him if we could cut some trees. He said, "No problem, we live in a forest and we have plenty of trees."

Well, we had seen three real nice-looking trees close to the village and we cut them and brought them in to make the bunker. When the village chief saw them, though, he said, "No, no, you cannot do this! Everything is wrong." We finally found out what was going on.

We had cut the betel nut trees. It was difficult to make up for what we had done, because the villagers would have to go a much greater distance to find a source of their drugs. But it taught me how a lack of knowledge about a culture can get you in trouble.

Training the Montagnards and other indigenous and ethnic troops had some other challenges, too, especially because of the language barriers. Each Montagnard village spoke its own dialect, the ethnic Vietnamese had their own language, and there might be French mixed in with both of these groups, so we had to use translators to communicate. This was difficult enough with one interpreter, super difficult with two, and sometimes we had to have three interpreters—one for each language. You might go from Montagnard to Vietnamese then Vietnamese to English or French. When a message got back to you, it was not always the same as when it started out because it got lost or changed in translation. It was kind of like playing a game of rumor.

That meant we sometimes had to rely on visual directions, but we didn't have blackboards or anything like that, so we would draw pictures in the dirt or use sandpaper on a blanket. The sandpaper was like Velcro, and we could paste things up to show them pictures.

Radio training was especially difficult, particularly when we tried to train them to understand the different radio frequency bands, so we often found ourselves using the Montagnards' form of communication, done by hitting pieces of bamboo against something. Depending on the length and width of the bamboo, it could make different sounds.

That worked pretty well, especially at night when we could use the bamboo signals to communicate with different posts around the village area. When the bamboo sounded at one place, the others had to answer with their bamboo to confirm they were awake and doing what they were supposed to be doing.

Another problem we had was that not all Montagnards were on our side. The Viet Cong and North Vietnamese did get to some tribes before we did and convinced them to join their cause.

Another problem we faced with all the troops we were training was that you couldn't always tell whose side they were on, something I began to be good at spotting as I did training with them. If one of the individuals I was training was a little too good at what we were doing or was learning a little bit too fast, especially if I was showing him something new, I could be pretty sure he was getting training elsewhere. A lot of us called these soldiers "doubtfuls," and we knew they were probably siding with the North Vietnamese or Viet Cong, which meant they were probably infiltrators. This happened consistently and in large numbers, and I saw it on all my tours in Vietnam.

On my first patrol after getting to Gia Vuc, I also began to see how the Viet Cong operated and how closely they were tied to the villages and the local soldiers we were training. When I went out on that patrol I was with some of the old trusted Vietnamese special forces people and about thirty or forty indigenous personnel.

The Vietnamese always liked to stop at about eleven in the morning to cook rice for lunch, and then they would rest and not start back on patrol until about three in the afternoon. At about ten that morning a few rounds were fired at us, way over our heads with no significant damage whatsoever, but we knew some Viet Cong were trying to let us know we'd made contact. That did not, however, stop the lunch break at eleven, and at some point I got to looking and realized we had a larger number of CIDGs at lunch than I originally had brought with me. I found out later that those extra guests were the Viet Cong who had fired at us earlier. The enemy had come in and had lunch with us.

I had several words with our LLDB counterparts and that put a stop to the free-lunch crowd, but this was a valuable lesson in how closely the Viet Cong were tied into the South Vietnamese villages, and how hard it was to tell who was a friend and who was an enemy in Vietnam.

We were especially at risk from the Viet Cong when we had to go out on the roads, which happened fairly often because we had to resupply the camp using roads out of the mountain jungle area down into Quang Ngai City. When we took old deuce-and-a-half World War II trucks down those roads to purchase or receive supplies from ships and deliver them back over the same road to the camp, we had a number of close calls.

On one trip, another American Special Forces soldier and I were stopped on our way back to the camp by a little local Viet Cong guerilla force that the North Vietnamese were developing to harass us. These VC were young, and at that time they did not have much infrastructure to communicate with their higher-ups, which later changed when the regular North Vietnamese Army infiltrated the country.

They stopped us by burning a little bridge and damaging it enough that we didn't think we could get across it with our heavy load of supplies, which included rice, pigs, and chickens we were taking back to the camp for food, so we stopped.

The six or eight little young Montagnard Viet Cong who were there decided they wanted some American prisoners, and they had their rusty-looking weapons right on us. Once they had us, though, they didn't know what to do with us, and they were having trouble getting in touch with their higher-ups.

It was around lunchtime when they stopped us, and knowing there was nothing the Montagnards liked better than cooking rice and having a party, the other sergeant and I decided to cook a little of the rice we had on our trucks while we were waiting. We also noticed that the Montagnards had a big old urn filled with their homemade liquor, and we decided that was pretty good, but we wanted to show them something better.

On board the truck we had some grape Kool-Aid that we put in the local water supply at the camp—and I mean that water was too thick to drink and too thin to plow—so the Kool-Aid really helped. We also got to looking around on our truck and found some 180-proof grain alcohol—that's double the strength of what you can buy in the United States—so we poured that 180 alcohol into the grape Kool-Aid, and it wasn't too bad. I tried some of it myself.

Well, this was about one-hundred-degree weather and about 90 to 95 percent humidity, and soon those young VC soldiers started helping us out on the grape Kool-Aid. Before long a couple of them got real sleepy and some of the others got real friendly and wanted to try some more of the Kool-Aid.

We also decided to help them out with their weapons, which were old and rusty and of several different calibers. We started showing them how to take them apart and clean them, and the little VC were amazed we knew how to handle them. Of course, occasionally we'd leave a part out as we put them back together.

The bottom line is that after several hours of drinking our Kool-Aid in that heat, most of the Viet Cong soldiers were completely passed out, and the remaining ones who were still fairly sober decided we were not bad people, so they helped us push the trucks across the dilapidated bridge and we were gone back to camp. We did leave them a little bit of the Kool-Aid, though.

The funny part about this was that the other sergeant and I didn't dare tell the camp commander what we had done, but because of the incident we were a full day late getting back to camp. When we got back, the camp commander told us that a reprimand would be put in our records. I guess somewhere the word got out about what happened, though, and the commander must have heard the story. A letter of reprimand never did get in our records.

The other thing about that tour was that threats didn't just come from the enemy. One of those times when we were making a trip for supplies, I was driving one of those deuce and a halfs loaded down with indigenous personnel and supplies when an armed US aircraft came over us. The plane turned and came right down on a May Day run straight at us, ready with its weapons, ready to blow us off of the road.

I realized what was happening and I happened to have the top down on my truck, so I stood up and took my hat off, waved it, and did everything I could to let him know we were Americans. There was no code to use for that, just signal as best we could and hope he recognized us, or that he would get close enough to tell we were Americans, not North Vietnamese or Viet Cong.

Right at the last minute the pilot went right up above us, wiggled his wings, and went on his way. He finally did recognize us, but for a while there I thought our own aircraft was going to blow us away.

That was just another day at the office, but that was one of my last trips to pick up supplies by truck, because after that our supplies were brought in by military and Air America aircraft. These aircraft sometimes landed at the camp to unload the supplies, and other times they would low-lex the supplies. "Low-lex" was short for low-altitude parachute extraction, a system where they would have supplies on pallets and have a big parachute attached to the pallets. The aircraft would fly real low and be just about ready to touch down, then the crew would push the pallets out and a chute would come open and pull those pallets right out of the rear of the aircraft, so the pilot never had to land.

They'd sometimes low-lex livestock, too, and this is where I got in a little bit of trouble. The weather had been real wet and we didn't have anything except a dirt landing strip. It got a little dangerous for them to land, and evidently they were running short on parachutes, so they couldn't drop the livestock. They radioed to ask what to do, and because we were in dire need of food, I said, "Drop them." They said, "We can't, we

don't have any parachutes" and I said, "Drop them anyway."
They did.

I figured there wasn't much difference whether you dropped
a cow with a parachute and slaughtered it right there for food,
or dropped it without a parachute and then you wouldn't have
to kill it yourself. That was not considered the American way,
though, and I got a little reprimand for that, but we did get
some food.

It was on that first trip that I also got a little wounded when
I ran a punji stick through my foot. A punji is a piece of green
bamboo the Viet Cong sharpened into a stake or spear, and
usually they would put them in with their pigs and other animals to cover them in bacteria, so whoever stepped on one
would get an infection. They would place these on a trail or
they would hide them on the side of the trail, and fire a weapon
toward the trail, causing us to run into them as we got away
from the gunfire. Sometimes they would put them in a hole
which, if you stepped in it, was hard to get out of without in-
juring yourself worse. These punjis weren't supposed to kill
us, just slow us down and cause us to get infections.

I was fortunate enough to have a medic on the site when
I stepped on this one. He took a metal weapon cleaning rod,
sterilized it, put a swab on one end, and ran it through my foot.
Then he put a Band-Aid on each side of the wound, gave me
some antibiotics, and said, "Go back to it." In no time at all, I
was back at forward duty.

That punji wound meant a Purple Heart for me, but otherwise I didn't have a whole lot of trouble on my first visit to
Vietnam, and I left there after about one hundred eighty days
with very few injuries.

CHAPTER FOUR

A GODFORSAKEN PLACE

I N LATE SUMMER OF 1965, when I went back to Vietnam for my second tour, I was sent to help provide security around the C Team headquarters in Nha Trang, the 5th Special Forces headquarters located in I Corps.

During the Vietnam War, South Vietnam was divided into four Corps Tactical Zones, each of which served as a command center for American and South Vietnamese forces. These included I Corps (also called "Eye" Corps), which covered the northernmost region of South Vietnam along the border of North Vietnam; II Corps, which was located in Pleiku and covered the Central Highlands Region north of Saigon, South Vietnam's capital city (now called Ho Chi Minh City); III Corps, which was located in Saigon and covered the region surrounding that area; and IV Corps, which covered the southernmost part of South Vietnam and the Mekong Delta and was based in Can Tho.

I wasn't in Nha Trang long, though, until my sergeant major came after me and said, "I want you to be my intel sergeant at C Team in Da Nang."

Now keep in mind that C Team, commanded by Lieutenant Colonel Kenneth B. Facey, was rear echelon. They got to sleep in beds, they had warm food, and they even had somebody to help shine their boots and do their laundry for them.

I said, "I can handle that. I'm ready. I'll be there."

But when I arrived in Da Nang about two days later, the sergeant major said, "I've got bad news for you. Ol' Sergeant Earl Petty out of the A-102 was hit and we had to medevac him out of the country yesterday. I'm going to have to send you out there as the intel sergeant."

"Out there" was an A Team camp in the middle of the A Shau Valley (*A Sầu* in Vietnamese), a narrow cut in the mountainous region of the Thua Thien Province of I Corps, just a few miles from the Laotian border. The valley is about thirty miles long, and at the time it was crisscrossed with many paths and trails. It was also one of the main routes the North Vietnamese were using to bring equipment, supplies, and troops into South Vietnam from North Vietnam and Laos, and it eventually became part of the Ho Chi Minh Trail that ran from North Vietnam through Cambodia and Laos and into South Vietnam.

Because this area was critical to the North Vietnamese, it was a hotbed of activity and conflicts that had a bad reputation among American troops. The bottom line is that, before I left for A Shau, I knew I was going into a bad location, but when I got on the ground there, I found out it was a terrible location.

When I arrived at A Shau, the camp was short three Americans—we just had two Special Forces officers and seven enlisted personnel—and over the weeks to come most of those Americans rotated out and were replaced by new men. Our medic, Sergeant First Class Vernon Carnahan, and our demolitions-engineering specialist, Wayne Murray, were both there when I arrived. By February of 1966, our team consisted of me, Carnahan, and Murray, and six fairly new men: Captain Davis Blair, our commanding officer; second in command, Lieutenant Lewis A. Mari; and enlisted men Master Sergeant Robert Gibson, Sergeant Owen McCann, Specialist Phillip Stahl, and Specialist George Pointon.

I can tell you that none of us were happy to be in that camp; it was about thirty miles from another friendly camp, was bordered by high mountains on the east and west, and was surrounded by a triple-canopy jungle. We were like fish in a barrel.

The site had been chosen because of its proximity to an airstrip, built with PSP, pierced (sometimes called "perforated") steel-plate panels that could be interlocked to create a road or an airstrip or to form walls, roofs, and other structures. These panels—also called Marston Mats because they had been developed in Marston, North Carolina, just before World War II as a quick way to build runways—were fifteen inches wide and eight or ten feet long, and had three-inch holes in them called "lightening holes" because they reduced the amount of steel in the panel and made them lighter.

Like many CIDG camps, A Shau was set up as a triangle to make it more defensible. Each side was about two hundred yards long, and the airstrip ran approximately north to south along the base of the triangle and near the camp's main gate.

The walls around the camp were made from dirt reinforced with tin, PSP, logs, and sandbags. Parts of the north and south walls were double walls, and the rest were single walls. Trenches ran along each wall, and there were drainage ditches that bisected the camp, running north to south and east to west.

Many of the camp's structures were in a deteriorated state, mostly because of the climate, though we did have a new concrete bunker near the camp's southwestern tip, another new one in the northwest portion of the camp, and a third bunker under construction near the south wall, fairly close to our water tower.

We Americans were mostly positioned in this southwest section of the camp where our team house, commo bunker, the dispensary, an 81 mm mortar pit, and other bunkers and supply rooms were located. The LLDB men were headquartered at the southwestern tip of the triangle near our area, and the CIDG forces were billeted throughout the camp.

The American team house, the center of our operations and where we ate and slept, had a thatch roof with a dirt floor and rattan sides sandbagged up to about waist high.

We slept on cots and under mosquito netting, and we had plenty of room around our cots for our footlockers, equipment, and personal effects. While some of the other soldiers had photos and other personal items in their areas, I didn't because those kinds of things could help someone identify me, so for security reasons I thought it was better not to keep them around.

In our footlockers we all had tiger-stripe jungle fatigues and some regular fatigue uniforms, though we didn't wear the regular fatigues too often. We didn't wear too many underclothes, either, because they didn't work very well in that hot, humid environment. But we all had a couple of sets of the lightweight, black pajamas commonly worn in Vietnam, which we usually slept in because we almost always had to get up at night when a round came in. That happened pretty frequently, and when it did we had to be up and gone. Our weapons were always close by our cots, and always ready in case we had to go to our assigned alert positions.

We all brought helmets with us, though we rarely wore those because they were hot and also because they were metal; if you hit that helmet against a tree or limb or accidentally tapped your weapon against it, it made a sound like no other in the jungle. Instead, we mainly wore the floppy boonie hats most of South Vietnam's indigenous soldiers used, though inside ours we always sewed a piece of international orange cloth we could use to signal an aircraft.

On one end of the team house we had a kitchen where we ate our meals, and this was the center of our social network where some people would play pinochle and poker. If anyone came to visit, that's where they would go and that's where we held all our meetings.

Another of the buildings in our part of the camp was supposedly the headquarters building, but it had a basement, so this became the underground dispensary. The dispensary had several cots, surgical equipment, and a large number of supplies for treating wounds and other ailments. Our medics in Vietnam could practice more advanced medicine there than would be allowed in the United States, to include surgery, so it was well stocked. Or we thought it was well stocked, because we were not expecting a couple of hundred patients.

We Americans did have our own cook, who we hand-picked for security reasons: after an incident during my first tour in Vietnam when a cook put glass shards in our food, I knew you couldn't be too careful.

We ate a lot of rice and vegetables (mostly bok choy) and some canned rations when we were in camp. We also had eggs, usually duck eggs, though we had very little poultry to eat. I remember one time when we were down to very little food there was some talk about eating the ducks, but that would mean we would have no more eggs, so the ducks stayed.

Pork and beef were the main livestock we had access to. For seasoning we had hot peppers and *nuoc mam*, fermented fish sauce called "armpit sauce" by many, which was horrible smelling, but it was hot (flavorwise) and filled with protein.

Water was not a problem for us in the camp because we had a well and a windmill. We could also take showers by filling a big, heavy-duty, rubber collapsible petroleum bladder with water and letting it sit long enough to warm up, which didn't take long in that weather. The water from the well was supposed to be drinkable, but we still treated it before we drank it. When we went on patrol, we could rely on the area streams, but we took tablets along to treat that water, too.

One big problem with Camp A Shau was its complete isolation. At one time, there had been another camp north of us in A Luoi, and there had been outposts on both of the mountains that came up on the east and west side of the camp, but those were not occupied. We just did not have enough people to man those outposts, because our forces in the camp had dwindled.

Because we were so far from civilization and there were no roads into the area, all of our supplies were delivered to us by air from C Team headquarters. These were not only war supplies, like ammunition, but basic supplies, too, like clothing and food for everyone in the camp—us Americans, the LLDB and CIDG men, and civilians alike.

It was not uncommon that resupply planes could not land because of the weather, and the weather was always a constant problem for us, almost like another enemy. At dusk on most nights, a thick fog would settle around us and not lift until after seven in the morning. And when rainstorms came in and stayed for days, that brought cloud ceilings down to zero above the valley floor and often delayed our air resupply.

Rain also caused problems for the airstrip, which would sometimes be too wet and soggy for planes to safely land. When that happened, sometimes we tried to fix it, like the time Wayne Murray took matters into his own hands. I was not there the day this happened, but Murray told me about it later.

"The drainage had gotten bad and water was getting under the runway, so when a plane would land, it would bog down," he said. "Captain Blair asked me if I could do something about that, so I took two cases of military dynamite out there, put a charge down, and hooked it all together with a det [detonation] cord. For some reason, instead of using an electrical firing system, I used a nonelectric one, and I cut myself about two minutes' worth of fuse, ignited it, jumped in the jeep, and drove back to the entrance of the camp."

As he got to the entrance, though, Murray said he looked up to see an Otter airplane coming in downwind.

"Blair saw it, too, and asked me if I had set off the charge," said Murray. "I said, 'Yeah.'"

"Can you stop it?" Blair asked.

"No."

According to Murray, they didn't have a radio with them to communicate to the Otter pilot, so Blair started to run to the commo shack, but Murray knew there was no way Blair would make it in time to warn the pilot off.

"I thought, 'Oh man, I'm going to go to jail,'" Murray recalled. "It turned out the pilot was about twenty feet off the ground when the charge went off. The aircraft rocked up on one wing and its other wing tip almost touched the ground when the pilot kicked it over and landed."

Murray remembered that the pilot stepped out of the plane, which now had big clods of red clay stuck on the underside of its wings, and asked, "Anyone have any clean underwear?"

"I never found out who that pilot was, but he sure had a lot of presence," said Murray of that pilot. "And I thought, 'I am going to become an army airplane pilot one day.'"

The camp was surrounded by five rows of defensive concertina wire and fields of claymore mines, some of which we had laid, and others that were left over from previous occupants. I am not sure it was really worthwhile to us to set those mines, though, because elephant grass, which was tall and had sharp leaves and grew in the open areas around the camp, would grow over the mined areas and we couldn't keep them clean. We had some people blown up when they tried to mow those areas, and any kind of animal wandering through would set them off.

The terrain above the valley floor was tough. Murray once described it as "uphill, downhill, uphill, downhill."

"Every time you'd go downhill you'd slip, start to slide, and you'd grab a tree and it would have thorns on it," he said. "Or every time you thought you'd gotten good at walking through the jungle, a vine would wrap around your ankle and throw you on the ground."

We had to deal with the wildlife there, too. Mosquitoes were always bad, but leeches were the worst. There were two kinds of leeches, dryland and water leeches, and we called them all bad names. I can't repeat them; they were that bad. And there were all kinds of monkeys, too, which some men kept as pets but a lot of us hated. Of course, there were a lot of other animals, including tigers, but we rarely saw those. We also had snakes, most of them poisonous, or the big constrictor kinds.

Nighttime patrols were always a challenge, not just because of the animals and plants, but because it was so dark in a triple-canopy jungle. Your eyes could get used to it, but you sure couldn't use a flashlight, so all you could do was feel your way around and try to get where you wanted to go, settle in, and wait for enough daylight to see.

One of the biggest problems in the camp was the attrition within our ranks. We could not keep the CIDG soldiers there. Anytime one of them had an injury or could talk a medic into giving them a trip out, they would leave and not return. Some of them just slipped away.

Of course, part of our problem with the CIDG men was that they were not exactly the cream of the crop. As Dave Blair once said, "They didn't send their best and brightest out to A Shau." A number of them were actually petty criminals given the choice of being sent to A Shau or going to jail, though after they got there I imagine jail might have looked pretty good. We also lost a few from NVA snipers.

George Pointon said he knew exactly what he was getting into when he came to the camp. That's because, on one of his earlier deployments to Vietnam, he was part of a team sent in to look for Special Forces campsites in the area.

"We were looking at five different potential locations for camps in the A Shau valley," he said, "and we had ordered them from the best locations to the worst. The irony is that some moron picked the one location that we had said, 'Don't, under any circumstances, put the camp there.' That's where they put it. I guess that's because they decided it was a place they could really piss the enemy off."

Wayne Murray told me later about arriving at the camp a few months before me, in August 1965, and what he thought as he looked down on it for the first time from the air. "Here's this camp at the bottom of a valley with hills on the east and west sides of it," he said. "I thought, 'This is going to be like Custer. We're going to sit there and all the Indians in the world are going to run right over us.'"

CHAPTER FIVE

THE MEN WITHIN THE WALLS

T**HOUGH IT WAS IN POOR CONDITION,** Camp A Shau was a busy place that operated 24/7, which was a challenge since, in the weeks before it was attacked, the camp contained less than three hundred personnel instead of the more than four hundred it should normally house.

In early March 1966, we had 210 CIDG soldiers, 41 civilian laborers, 10 civilian prisoners, 6 LLDB special forces soldiers, 2 interpreters, and 9 of us American Special Forces soldiers.

The South Vietnamese LLDB company commander in the camp was First Lieutenant Chung Uy Dung, who was supposed to lead his own South Vietnamese special forces men as well as the three CIDG companies in the camp—companies 121, 131, and 141. But Dung was not a very good commander, and it showed in how his men and the CIDG soldiers worked in the camp, such as when we were trying to get them out on patrol.

I could get full cooperation from Dung and the other LLDB leaders when we were planning the patrols, but implementing them was another story. If I wanted a patrol to leave early in the morning, say about six, I would be lucky to even get an LLDB leader up, much less have the patrol ready. Even though the LLDB commanders were supposed to be commanding them and we were only supposed to be advising, most of the time we Americans were doing their work for them. At A Shau, we were no longer just advisors; we were doing it all.

What this entailed was that, before we went out on patrol, I had to make sure the men had all the equipment they needed for the operation, including any necessary food and water, and I had to inspect everything to be sure the equipment was serviceable. I always made them jump up and down and move around to see that there were no metal-on-metal sounds that would give them away in the jungle.

A lot of times, when I finally got some of them out of camp to start the patrol, half of them would still be in camp. Then I would go in to get the stragglers, and part of the others would come back in. They just didn't go until they got ready.

Blair recalled that when he got to A Shau in February 1966, he could tell immediately that the men behind the walls were in as bad shape as the walls themselves. But he chalked some of that up to the conditions we were all living in at the camp.

"The isolation of the camp itself was depressing," he said. "There was no contact with any outside world, and there was nothing in range of us if we needed help. No artillery, no friendly units that were anywhere near being able to provide support or assistance to us. The camp's men were in a state of collective paranoia. I suppose anyone in that state of isolation would be that way."

Murray, who had been there a long time, thought it was less about their mental health than it was about the quality of the men and where their loyalties lay.

"A Shau was kind of a unique camp," Murray said, "because, unlike most CIDG camps, the indigenous Montagnards who lived around there were pro–North Vietnamese. They were part of the enemy. And I never had a whole lot of trust in a lot of the South Vietnamese soldiers there, either. Some of them were great, some were NVA sympathizers, and some were just shiftless criminals."

Whatever the reason, those soldiers were difficult to train and motivate, and they were not too concerned with tactics, either. When we were out on patrol, it was hard to get them to do anything but walk behind one another, which just made a trail that anyone could follow. We also had to show them how to make their way through the jungle vegetation, which you had to part by hand rather than hack, because cutting it made a distinct sound that was not good tactically.

And they didn't pay attention too well. One time I was out on patrol with an LLDB squad leader and a full company of ninety to one hundred CIDG men. They were going through the jungle making all kinds of noise, and I was bringing up the rear when I looked over off the trail, and by a tree stood a Montagnard warrior—long hair, loincloth, crossbow, and so forth. I took the guy by surprise when I said "*Van didi*," which is "Good day, sir" in the Laotian language. It scared him so much that he dropped his crossbow and disappeared.

47

He was probably a member of the Katu tribe that lived in that area of Vietnam's Central Highlands, and was one of those tribes that never became friendly with the Special Forces the way other tribes had. Many of these Katu had joined with the Viet Cong, who used them to track us down, and when they ran you, they ran you hard.

One thing was for sure, the Katu were much better in the jungle than the CIDG men. That whole group of one hundred or so people had walked by him and he was close enough to reach out and touch them, but they never saw him.

We also ran into that same old problem about how the mainstream Vietnamese treated Montagnards. I remember one operation where recon teams had seen some kind of signal on a mountain, and we took a patrol up there to check it out. We made it to the mountain with no problems after walking all day, but as we went on top of the mountain, the first indigenous point person, who was a Montagnard, was shot.

It didn't kill him, but the medevac helicopter we called in was flown by a South Vietnamese pilot who, when he found out it was a Montagnard that had been shot, refused to come in and pick him up. The pilot claimed it was because the conditions were unsafe, but that was just an excuse.

The Montagnard died before we got him back to camp by land, which probably could have been prevented if they had picked him up and gotten him to a medical facility. There was not a thing I could do about that kind of discrimination except make a report, but it was hard for me and the other Special Forces men to comprehend when they were all supposed to be on the same team.

The CIDG men also did dumb things that risked their own lives. For example, one night when I was out with a patrol, I found two of the indigenous soldiers smoking cigarettes, which endangered everyone and completely ruined the mission. I reported it to Dung when we got back in camp, but he just shrugged it off, saying, "It's going to happen."

Thankfully, we didn't get anyone killed that time, but it should never have happened. They should have known the enemy could smell the smoke or see the cigarettes burning. That and other training issues were also things the LLDB men should have handled, but it almost always fell to us Americans.

A lot of these patrols were unsuccessful because of the performance of our CIDG troops, who often did everything in their power to avoid making contact with the enemy. But we did have some successful patrols when we were able to kill some enemy or, better yet, capture them, usually by wounding them. We were fortunate when this happened, because we could usually get them to talk by making them think they were not going to receive medical attention unless they did talk. Of course, sometimes what they told us was valuable and sometimes it was not.

We also had some success performing other parts of our jobs, such as reconnaissance from helicopters or fixed-wing aircraft. One way we did this was to hitch a ride on any type of aircraft that came into camp and have them fly over the area, so we could see what was happening in the jungle below us. On one of those trips I had a little incident, though.

I was in a small fixed-wing aircraft, and we were flying over the jungle when we spotted a large enemy force, which we didn't know at that time was a full division of fully trained North Vietnamese soldiers, but we knew it was a larger force than anyone expected.

Well, the pilot got a little too close to the enemy on that run and they shot us down. That little ol' pilot bounced us off the top of the jungle, about fifty to sixty yards the first time. When we hit the second time, we fell through the canopy a little and bounced again about half that distance. The third time we bounced all the way down into the canopy, rolled over, and all we had to do was step out in the canopy and drop down about four feet and we were on the ground.

We were lucky because, whether he meant to or not, the pilot had maneuvered us far enough away from where we were shot that the North Vietnamese didn't know where to look for us. Our guys came out and picked us up and we walked away without so much as a scratch.

We also sometimes were able to interdict (a military term for disrupting or destroying enemy forces or supplies en route to the battle area). Most of the time we didn't have enough troops or forces to interdict a major convoy, but we could make some progress with some of the smaller elements, though normally when this happened we had to hit the target, do what we were going to do, and run hard to get away because we knew they were going to reinforce.

CHAPTER SIX

BOOTS ON THE GROUND; SIGNS IN THE JUNGLE

AS BAD AS CAMP A SHAU'S structural and personnel conditions were, we were evidently doing fairly well at our jobs because, during my first one hundred or so days in camp, it seemed like the enemy shot at me every day. Of course, at the time I didn't know it, but maybe they were just zeroing-in their weapons for what was to come.

What I did know was that we were getting information that indicated a big buildup of NVA forces around us. Some of that information came from a patrol Dave Blair was on not long after he got to A Shau in February.

The patrol, which had been in an ambush skirmish earlier that morning, set up a perimeter at about eleven o'clock to eat lunch. Because of the ambush, though, Blair was being careful, and he sent a small recon team forward to a stream crossing to check things out.

"The team ran across an NVA soldier taking a crap, pants off and all," said Blair. "We were all starting to eat our rice balls when we heard this shooting, and all [of] the sudden this guy came running into our area wearing a shirt and naked on the bottom. He saw us and started spraying us with his AK-47, his bullets flying all around, and everybody started shooting inside the perimeter."

According to Blair, no one was hit in that skirmish, but they did find some documents in the man's pants, and between those and some other documents we got from another NVA soldier who had been killed by a patrol, we were able to get an idea of the reconnaissance the enemy was doing on us.

In addition to our patrol and recon missions providing good information about what the enemy was up to, we could also hear what they were doing. You see, we were so far out in the jungle that sound carried a long way. At night, over the sound of insects and other animals, I could hear large convoys of trucks going. I reported their coordinates to higher head-quarters, but they didn't believe it because there were no roads in the A Shau Valley.

What they didn't realize was the North Vietnamese were building a series of roads under A Shau's triple canopy. Even though we in the camp knew it, we didn't have a large enough force to interdict those convoys, so all we could do was keep listening and reporting what we heard. And we were realizing one thing for sure—the NVA forces around us were getting larger.

There were also other signs that should have warned me about the trouble we were going to face, including the loyalties of some of our CIDG forces. I wish I had paid more attention to those signs.

For example, one night when I was with elements of the 141 Company doing security detail outside the camp, our group of about twenty was in a ditch at the south end of the airstrip when six or eight North Vietnamese soldiers came up on high ground waving and talking. We could see them and it would have been easy to kill some or all of them. We were definitely in kill ratio, and I was locked and ready to fire when the 141 commander grabbed me by the shoulder and said, "No fire."

I thought at the time it was a tactical decision on his part not to fire on that group and maybe he knew there were many more of the enemy out there, enough to overcome our twenty men on the patrol, so I didn't question him. But, instead of staying out the rest of the night, I had them move the company back into the camp because I knew we were compromised. I did make a report on the incident, but there were no repercussions.

So all we could do was keep an eye on things, report back to our higher-ups, and hope we were not going to be trapped in that jungle valley.

CHAPTER SEVEN

THE GATHERING STORM

W E HAD KNOWN FOR WEEKS that something was happening around us, but it was not until March 5 that we really understood how bad our situation was.

I had been out on patrol that day with some of the 141 Company and we ran up on an NVA outpost, a thatch hut, what we called a "hooch," with some of their equipment in it. I wanted to take the equipment and burn the hooch, but the Vietnamese officer leading the patrol wouldn't let me because, I assumed, he thought it might let the NVA know where we were. But I learned the real reason after we got a call to come back to camp immediately. While we were out, two North Vietnamese soldiers had walked into our camp and given themselves up.

The two men were dressed in khaki and had walked out of the elephant grass and onto the airstrip in front of a jeep driven by one of our unarmed civilian mechanics. The mechanic brought them into camp without a problem, though, because these guys wanted to be taken prisoner. They had had enough of life in the jungle, and they did not want to be killed in the battle they knew was coming. I guess they decided it was better to participate in the Chieu Hoi amnesty program, which the South Vietnamese military had developed to encourage Viet Cong and other enemy combatants to defect to the ARVN side.

Dave Blair recalled that their arrival in camp brought on a lot of celebration among our troops. As the O&I sergeant, I helped interrogate the defectors before they were taken on to higher headquarters for more in-depth questioning, and we were able to find out a lot from them that helped us realize what we were facing. I don't recall all the details from their interrogations, but years later Dave Blair got ahold of the declassified records from one of those men, Ngyuen Tien Dung, who at the time was about twenty-six years old and was a sergeant in the North Vietnamese Army.

Dung had been drafted six years before and had worked his way up through the ranks to be a sergeant in the NVA's 95th Regiment, 325th Division, which had received orders to infiltrate into South Vietnam in December 1965. His battalion left North Vietnam on December 23, 1965, and spent some forty days traveling on mountain trails through Laos and into the A Shau Valley. By the time Dung defected, the regiment was situated about six miles northwest of our camp.

Dung told us that he had been lied to by his leaders, who had claimed that South Vietnam was already 45 percent liberated. By the time they got to A Shau Valley, Dung realized he had been misled. He had also gotten tired of the hardships he was experiencing—the lack of food, clothing, and medicine and the generally poor living conditions for the soldiers. Dung had decided he no longer believed in the Communist cause, so he and his fellow defector had slipped away from their squad while their platoon was eating the evening meal.

Both men gave us a good bit of information about the size of their forces, the weapons they were carrying, and the plans the enemy had for Camp A Shau. The bottom line was that the NVA's 325th Infantry Division was all around us and ready to attack. Their plan was to hit us beginning on March 11 or 12, when the weather was supposed to turn bad and could give cover to the NVA as they set up positions around our camp, while also keeping us from getting air support.

"These defectors didn't make any bones about it," said Blair. "They said their battalion was part of a regiment that had been assigned to attack our camp and they were going to do it as soon as the weather turned."

Around the time the defectors came in, George Pointon began reporting some other bad signs. He had found places in the concertina wire that had been pushed down, no doubt by the enemy who were watching or probing the camp. He also found a series of lead wires in an area outside the camp. These leads, he said, had been made out of our US-authorized commo wire and they all came off of a main line, or "trunk." He figured out the leads were being used by the NVA to find their way in the dark to and from locations around the camp.

Curious about those wires, Pointon said he went out of the camp one day, leaving his weapon behind, and began to follow one of the wires, which led to a ditch. Pointon kept walking past the ditch and recognized it was a trail made by people coming back and forth to the camp, but it was not a trail our patrols had made.

"Suddenly, I was seeing places out there where people had been sleeping and eating, like five minutes before," he said. "Then I realized I was out there without a weapon, and I was probably in the midst of the enemy."

Luckily, he made it back into camp without incident. "I guess they didn't want to do anything to me because they didn't want to give away their presence," he said.

Having learned from the North Vietnamese defectors that an attack was imminent, Blair began to ask for assistance from our higher-ups. On March 5, he requested reinforcements of at least two Marine, ARVN, or "Mike Force" rifle companies and at least two, though preferably a battery, of 105 mm howitzers. (Mike Force teams are what Dave Blair once described as "hybrid" Special Forces teams. They are a light infantry unit equipped and trained to operate in remote areas without any significant logistical requirements or support. These teams were often used for reinforcement of A camps under attack or under pressure of attack, which was our case, but they also gathered intelligence and worked to disrupt and stop Viet Cong and North Vietnamese activities in remote areas. Their operations might last a few days or over a month, but they could survive with no resupplies for however long they needed.)

"I was begging for reinforcements and I sent a sarcastic message asking for Mike Force or Marines or ARVN or WACS [Women's Army Corp] or anything," Blair said.

They did not send reinforcements, but they did send daily overflights, which were able to spot the enemy setting up fortifications north and south of the camp, and air strikes were delivered against several of these fortified areas, though they had little impact on the NVA's numbers or plans.

On March 7, our side dropped several thousand leaflets, used to encourage the NVA and VC to surrender, over the valley, and planes flying overhead broadcast loudspeaker appeals recorded by the two defectors encouraging their former colleagues to defect as well, but that didn't produce any results.

March 7 was also the day at least some help did arrive in the form of eight fresh Special Forces soldiers: a new weapons man for our A Team, Specialist Herril Robbins, and seven men from the A-503 Mike Force—Captain Tennis (Sam) Carter, Sergeant First Class Victor Underwood, Sergeant First Class Raymond Allen, Staff Sergeant Billie Hall, and Sergeants John Bradford, Minter Hoover, and Jimmy Taylor. With them were nine interpreters and more than 140 Chinese Nungs.

Mike Force teams were tough. And this team was especially good. According to Victor Underwood, Sam Carter had handpicked the team himself, and the Nungs they brought with them were also exceptional.

Nungs were Vietnamese tribesmen who originally came from the southern part of China and had found a niche for themselves in Vietnam as mercenaries. They had a reputation for being tough, fearless fighters, and they were also very loyal. Of course, they were pretty well paid, too—Nungs were paid better for their service than other Vietnamese minority groups. But they earned it. The Nungs were also helpful to us because they could understand radio communications from the North Vietnamese, which were sometimes spoken in Chinese. In my opinion, China was probably working with the North

Vietnamese, though I'm not sure that was ever officially confirmed. Keep in mind that the Mike Force team had not come to support us in a battle; they were there to pull security for us while the camp was being reinforced and rebuilt in preparation for a possible battle. They probably didn't know what they were getting into until they landed, either. But once they were on the ground they began to grasp the situation.

Victor Underwood remembered thinking, "Holy shit, we're going to need a lot more than 140 men." But they got to work setting up temporary fighting positions for themselves in the camp.

In the days leading up to the battle, the CIDG soldiers worked harder than usual helping fortify and prepare the camp, too, including cutting back the elephant grass from around the camp's perimeter, digging trenches, and sandbagging a gap in the south wall of the camp.

George Pointon recalled one CIDG guy who helped him on the south wall before and during the battle, a man he met under less than ideal conditions.

A few days before the battle, Pointon had caught this particular soldier stealing supplies from one of our storage units and had stopped him. The soldier threatened to go get a gun and shoot Pointon, but eventually he just slinked off.

The next morning, though, Pointon spotted the guy sitting with some other CIDG soldiers. "I figured they were probably talking about shooting me and I knew I had to mend some fences," he said. "I had a couple of canteens of hot chocolate with me and I walked over and handed him one of my canteens. He looked at me, took the hot chocolate, and essentially said everything was okay."

Later that day, Pointon invited the soldier, who he called Bao, to help reinforce part of the south wall, Pointon's combat position. Much to his surprise, Bao showed up with some other CIDG men and set to work.

As the camp prepared for the battle, Carter, Blair, and the LLDB captain, Dung, began developing a spoiling attack plan they hoped to launch against the enemy on March 10. They thought a raid against NVA fortifications in the southeast end of the valley would throw off the enemy and cause them to delay or call off the attack.

"It was really kind of stupid I suppose," said Blair, "but Sam and I knew the enemy was approaching and we knew things were getting rough. We thought they were digging in on our south side and we planned to do a World War I trench attack [a system of making small-scale nighttime surprise attacks on enemy positions]."

About this time, though, the weather changed—a few days earlier than we had expected—and with it came a humid, misty drizzle with no winds to blow the clouds away.

On March 8, I was out on another patrol that had gone south from the camp when we received a message on our CW (continuous wave) radio to come back to camp. Wayne Murray, who was on another patrol, got the call as well. A third defector had come into camp with news the attack was imminent.

Though our patrol had not made contact with any enemy at that time, as we came back into camp, we found more locations where the NVA had set up their staging areas getting ready to move their large force in.

That night, we were on general alert. We had already developed a plan of action in case we were attacked, but the plan had not included the Mike Force, so we had to adjust it to make sure they and the Nungs had firing positions. We also went back over it to make sure everyone knew what they were supposed to do.

After that, I went to our ammo storage and put more ammo at my alert position, the 81 mm mortar pit right outside the door of the team house.

The pit was not really a "pit" down in the ground, but instead it was closer to ground level. It was double-sandbagged around the outside and the base plates were cemented in, so it was set. There was enough room in there for four or five people, but whoever was in there would have to stay low, since it was more elevated than a normal mortar pit.

I had different aiming stakes set around to let me know the directions I was firing from, so I could be more accurate. We also put in a lot more illumination rounds, white phosphorous for spotting rounds, and the high-explosive rounds that would do the most damage. I put all I could in the area around my station and made sure the grenade sump, a little trench that gives protection if a live grenade comes into the pit, was open.

I also had a small FM radio in there I could use to communicate with all the other Americans around the camp, and another radio I could use to communicate with the support aircraft flying above us.

By dusk, the cloud ceiling had dropped to three hundred meters, at just about the same time an enemy squad was spotted at the north end of the airstrip.

We had a meal that night, though I can't recall what I ate, and we went to bed fully clothed, our gear and weapons close at hand, ready to leap out of bed at the first sign of attack. I don't think any of us slept, though, and all night long we listened to digging noises just outside the camp as the North Vietnamese soldiers began to set up their positions.

There would be no spoiling attack. Instead, just before dawn on March 9, 1966, we received a full-on attack from our enemies, the 325B Infantry Division.

CHAPTER EIGHT

BEFORE SUNRISE

T HE ATTACK BEGAN ABOUT three fifty in the morning with the sound of an artillery bombardment
Dave Blair later described as the "crumping" of
many rounds of mortar. Seconds later, though to many of us it
seemed like hours as we waited for them to explode, the shells
hit the camp. And they made direct hits on our team house,
the commo bunker, and other American buildings. The NVA
knew right where to find us thanks, no doubt, to NVA sympathizers or infiltrators in our camp.

In the midst of this horrible barrage of mortars and artillery
fire, I remember running straight from my bunk in the team
house to my alert position at my 81 mm mortar pit right outside the building.

Once I got there, my men and I immediately began firing
back with white phosphorous "Willie Pete" rounds—the kind

we used for destroying equipment or registering the indirect fire weapons—and high-explosive shells.

Dave Blair, who had been awake all night, was out checking the defenses on the south wall when he heard those first mortars, and he recalled he ran into the team house where he gathered up a 12-gauge pump shotgun, a bagful of shotgun shells, his rifle, a slew of magazines all loaded up, his .45 pistol, and his hand grenades. "Oh my God, I could hardly move. I must have had one hundred pounds of gear on me, and all of us were sort of loaded down like that," he said.

I had all my equipment, too, including a pump-action Winchester Model 12, which was faster than my automatic rifle. I had cut off the shotgun's barrel to make it more effective at close range and, while it did not have long-range value at all, it had proven to be very lethal for breaking up ambushes in the jungle. There is some question on the legality of it—I might have been using an unlawful weapon—but even if I had known that, it probably wouldn't have stopped me. I don't think the North Vietnamese signed the Geneva Convention.

That first barrage lasted until about six thirty-five that morning, and a lot happened in those few hours.

Wayne Murray recalled the start of the attack this way:

"We knew the attack was imminent, so I was lying in my bunk and I had my flack jacket on and my equipment was on the floor. All of a sudden I hear 'boom, boom, boom.' Mortar rounds going off. I rolled out and got my stuff and ran out to my position, a double berm with dirt pushed up against PSP and apertures that we could fire out of."

George Pointon, who had come into the camp in January, said he knew before the battle started that we were in for a bad fight, but how bad it was became super evident to him at that moment.

"When the battle got started, I knew right away that it was not going to go away," he said. "I knew that this guy [the enemy] wanted this valley, and he was not going to allow us to stay."

When the mortar fire started, Pointon was in the dispensary and watched as John Bradford, Billie Hall, and others took off ahead of him into the incoming mortar barrage. Pointon said he hesitated, waiting for some kind of lapse in the incoming fire before he went to his position on the south wall, and when a lapse finally occurred, he made a run for it.

"I no sooner left that bunker than a round came in, hit on the side of one of our tin utility shacks, and knocked me senseless," Pointon said. "I don't know how long I was there, but I woke up and my weapon was gone and there were still explosions going off."

He crawled around until he found his weapon, then attempted another run for his position, making it all the way this time. When he got there, Pointon said Bao and several other CIDG soldiers were already there, all of them fighting bravely as they tried to keep the NVA from coming in from the south side.

Pointon and the CIDG soldiers were very effective holding the south wall for as long as they could, killing a great number of NVA before they could breach the wall.

Unfortunately, not everyone was that successful. In fact, several of our casualties occurred in the first few minutes of the battle when we were going from our beds to our fighting positions, especially those whose positions were farther away than mine. That's what happened to Mike Force Sergeant

Raymond Allen and our A Team leader, Robert Gibson, who were both hit in the first minutes of the battle. I wasn't there to see that, but Vic Underwood was.

According to Underwood, who had also been sleeping in the dispensary, Bradford and Allen left first. Jimmy Taylor, Minter Hoover, Billie Hall, and Underwood started out after them, but they had to take cover from the mortar fire. When that barrage slacked off, Underwood started running toward the Nung positions, which were in trenches near the camp's north wall.

When he got just past the commo bunker, though, he found Gibson lying in the middle of the road that ran the length of camp, with a bad wound in the back of his head. Underwood thought he was dead until he heard Gibson groan, so he picked Gibson up and started dragging him to a Nung trench. At just about that time, another round came in, further wounding Gibson and knocking Underwood down, but once Underwood got his wind back, he picked Gibson up again and got him into the trench. In that trench, though, he found Bradford and Allen, both of them wounded: Allen was hit in the head and chest, Bradford in the leg, buttocks, and hand.

Gibson, like me, had run out of the team house toward the 81 mm mortar pit and was spun around by an explosion, which he later said did not seem particularly strong, but he did feel a sting in his right arm and on a front tooth. He stopped to feel the tooth, which broke off in his hand, and as he was putting it in his pocket he felt another explosion. After that, all he could remember was hearing Carnahan yell that he was coming to get him and then getting an injection from Carnahan. The next thing Gibson recalled was waking up in the hospital; he did not recall how he got there.

After making Allen as comfortable as possible, Underwood helped Bradford to the relative safety of the commo bunker, where Hoover was trying to get a message out to higher head-quarters. Underwood found medic Billie Hall and took him to the trench to help Allen and Gibson, then Vic ran back to the commo bunker to check on Bradford. About that time, another heavy barrage came in and, when Underwood returned to the trench, he found Allen's and Hall's interpreter dead and saw that Hall was badly injured. One of his legs was gone and the other one was mangled.

Underwood put tourniquets on Hall's legs there in the trench before he came and got me out of my mortar pit, and the two of us went back to the trench together to take care of Hall and Gibson. I gave Hall a shot of morphine while Under-wood tried to find bleeders inside Hall's legs and clamp them. But we couldn't stop the bleeding and we had no blood to give him for a transfusion, so all I could do was put an IV in his arm and give him some blood volume expander, the canned blood substitute we used in the field when a blood transfusion was impossible.

We finally got Hall and Gibson into the underground dispensary and saw that Gibson was shot up really bad.

"I was amazed to see him alive," recalled Dave Blair. "I've never seen more holes in a man."

This is when Hall's heroics happened. Even with his legs blown off and bleeding to death, he continued to advise the indigenous medics through an interpreter on how to treat the other wounded, dragging himself around the floor of the dispensary as he gave those instructions and only permitting the slightest treatment of his own wounds—just enough so he could live a little longer to direct operations at the aid station. Billie Hall died at about nine that morning.

By this time, the mortar barrage had slackened and those of us who were still on our feet began to assess the situation. One of the priorities was our water tower, which we knew we needed badly, and also knew that it had been hit because several people had seen the civilian who took care of the tower try to climb up and repair it.

According to Blair, as the civilian was climbing up the ladder, a sniper shot him right in the head. "It looked like a Hollywood movie," Blair said. "The guy fell from up toward the top of the ladder and his legs caught up in the ladder down below. He was just dead, hanging there all that time."

Wayne Murray recalled that incident, too. "I remember when he climbed up on the tower and a round cracked out and he fell backwards just like in a Wild West movie," he said. "I ran over there and he had been shot right in the forehead. I watched the lights go out in his eyes."

Our communications systems were also in a mess. Minter Hoover worked hard through all the fighting to repair some of our radios and communication lines, but the generators had been blown up so there was no power, antenna masts were blown off, wires were damaged, and most of the smaller radios we used for external communications with headquarters in Da Nang and Nha Trang were knocked out of commission by the blasts. The worst thing was that someone had cut the underground antenna with a knife, apparently sliced by one of our own people in the camp who must have been working for the other side.

Because the attack had happened so fast and because our outside communication systems were so badly damaged, we didn't have any way to let our higher headquarters in Da Nang and Nha Trang even know we were under attack until about 7:45 A.M., and it was an hour after that before our Detachment C-1 bosses in Da Nang actually heard the news. When they did hear about it, staff journal reports show I Corps Tactical Operations Center (TOC) called in an immediate air strike to assist us at 8:46 A.M. and an A-113 Nung force was put on standby for possible deployment, but at 8:50 a call came in from the 1st Division TOC at Hue—the weather would not permit any assistance at that time.

At 9:30 A.M., we were able to finally establish communication with the higher-ups through a CW radio, and we requested an emergency resupply of ammunition. By that time in the battle about half of our mortar ammo was gone, and a good bit of the machine gun ammo, too. We also needed a medical evacuation of the wounded, which included Gibson and Bradford, and reinforcements. But all we could do was wait and see what kind of help might arrive.

As Underwood was out in the camp assessing things, he started looking for Sam Carter, who no one had seen since the night before. According to Underwood, when he finally found Carter, the man looked a mess. "He was covered in dirt from head to foot. All I could see was his eyeballs," Underwood said.

Turned out that Carter had been sleeping in the supply room when the mortar fire began and it had collapsed on top of him. He had spent much of the day digging himself out of the rubble.

Throughout the day, the NVA's artillery and mortar barrages would heat up, then slack off, and they would send in groups of men to attack the camp.

Wayne Murray remembers being at his position fairly early that first morning and seeing sparks flying off the PSP. "I wondered what was going on and then I realized it was bullets hitting the PSP," said Murray. "I had put some claymore mines around the outside of the camp and when I pulled the det chord on those, I saw people go up in the air. The enemy was definitely inside that area of the camp perimeter."

Pointon said that he and the CIDG soldiers helping him on the south wall were also trying to keep these early attackers out and were using hand grenades on the charging NVA. They would wait until enemy soldiers were inside the concertina wire that surrounded the camp, then throw grenades at them.

"When we began throwing grenades, they started running back and forth because they had nowhere to go and we caught a lot of them out there," he said. "After that, we stashed hand grenades along the wall and kept lobbing them anytime we thought we saw some of them coming in, but after a while I realized that I was throwing a lot of grenades at dead bodies. You couldn't tell if they were dead or not, because you'd throw a grenade and the bodies bounced up and down. But I knew we couldn't waste the grenades, so we took a C ration box and started making a mark each time we shot one."

After Bradford was hit and taken to the medical bunker for treatment, Carter was given his rifle by members of the Nung Recon Platoon. Shortly thereafter, he was in a trench with Underwood and Carnahan when the three of them did something crazy. Underwood and Carnahan would stand up to draw enemy fire and then Carter, using Bradford's rifle, would head shoot them. They sure put a hurt on those NVA snipers.

Bradford told me later he lost the weapon after he was shot and evacuated, but he had etched his name on it somewhere, and when he was a commissioned officer serving later on a trip to Thailand and flying helicopters, the weapon showed up.

Things were tough, but all we could do was keep fighting, and I am sure some of us had moments when we wanted to stop.

Wayne Murray told me later these early hours of the battle taught him one big thing: "It doesn't matter how gung ho you are, or how well trained you are, in a battle there are some times you are going to be brave and there are some times you're going to have to sit and recover yourself."

Though he admitted there were times when he thought about slipping off into the elephant grass to hide until it was all over, he didn't. "The grass had too many bad guys in it," he said. "There were times when I was overwhelmed. I am sure there were times when others were overwhelmed, too. But you gather yourself back together and you continue to do your job. I'd think, 'If I live through this, I'm going to have to look in the mirror and shave for the rest of my life' and I didn't want to be looking at a coward."

CHAPTER NINE

HOPE AND HELL

DURING THE LULL in the mortar fire that morning, Wayne Murray went around the camp to check on the CIDG troops and found a lot of them badly injured, many with gut wounds. "There was nothing we could do for them," he said. We could only keep sitting and waiting.

At about eleven o'clock help finally began to arrive when navy pilots started dropping strikes on the north and south ends of the camp. This was not easy, since the low cloud cover and heavy ground fog meant the pilots couldn't see the targets and had to use sound to place them. That worked surprisingly well, but those of us in the camp held our breaths and hoped they hit the enemy and not us.

About the same time, two army aircraft came in to evacuate some of the wounded. They landed on the airstrip without drawing any enemy fire as they came in. It was amazing that those little ol' pilots got their small aircraft in through the bad weather and landed, and we began to move Gibson outside the camp to put him in the aircraft. We had the CIDG, a platoon from the Mike Force, and several Americans deployed around the airstrip to secure it, and initially there was no enemy resis-. tance, but once the aircraft landed, firing began. It was small-arms fire, but it was heavy and it was coming from the south half of the east wall. At first we thought the enemy had gotten between the east wall and the airstrip and that's who was firing at us, but then we realized the shots were coming from inside our camp, not outside.

That's when some of the Americans inside the camp saw that the 141 Company, stationed in that part of the camp, were firing at something. When they moved to that area to check it out, they realized the 141 Company was firing at us.

When the firing began, one of the pilots cranked up his plane and took off, but the other one stayed, and we managed to get Gibson on the plane by driving an old three-quarter or two-and-a-half-ton truck between the aircraft and the area where the shots were coming from. I had to pull a seat out of the airplane to shield Gibson and get him in the aircraft, and later I kidded him and told him there would be a statement of charges to him because he had to pay for the seat.

With the NVA firing on us from the outside and the 141 Company firing at us from the inside, Mari took a small force out to try to secure an area across the strip. Carter and Blair took cover behind a pile of fifty-five-gallon drums, though Blair recalled Carter had more drums to hide behind than he did.

"Sam got behind a bunch of barrels and I probably had one lousy barrel," said Blair. As they were exchanging fire with the enemy or the 141, Blair said Carter still found some humor in it. "With all that firing going on and them blazing away at us, Sam looked back at me and said, 'Ha, I got more barrels than you do.' I said, 'I wanna shoot you myself, Sam.'"

I was hit in the leg with a round during that time, and I know for sure it came from one of our supposed friendlies who had decided to fight with the other side. But the Mike Force eventually managed to stop them from firing on us, and at that point we needed to figure out what to do about them. We Americans wanted to disarm them, but there was some thought that the reason they were shooting at us was because it was an American who was being evacuated, not a wounded South Vietnamese, plus we needed all the firepower we could muster, so it was decided to let them keep their weapons. But there was no doubt the NVA had infiltrated the 141 Company, which meant one area of our compound was not defended properly, and the enemy was in the compound with us.

Though we asked for support both on the ground and from the air, we only got it from the skies.

At about one o'clock the cloud ceiling had lifted enough to let a Douglas AC-47 Spooky (also nicknamed "Puff the Magic Dragon"; the big gunship had a lot of firepower—the guns on those things could shoot six thousand rounds per minute in close air support) come in to support the camp. As it approached from the northwest and was passing on the west side of the camp, the people in the camp actually stood up and cheered and applauded as it arrived, thinking it would inflict a whole lot of damage on the enemy.

But before that could happen, the enemy opened up on it with a heavy and intense barrage of antiaircraft machine guns. That plane descended with a trail of smoke from the engine, circled south, and was still taking hits as it began to glide to the north, where it crashed in the valley about two miles from the camp. I later learned the enemy immediately began closing in on it, and four of the seven crewmen were killed before a CH-43 helicopter could come in and rescue the three remaining survivors. The AC-47 never even had a chance to fire its weapons, and the enemy captured two mini-guns and twenty-two thousand rounds of ammunition from it.

This was demoralizing for those of us in the camp, because we realized it meant the enemy could take out our reinforcements even if the weather was clear, and it meant we probably would not get the support we needed.

Luckily, we did get some resupply help that afternoon with three drops from single aircraft sorties that made low-level runs under the clouds from north to south, running the gauntlet of antiaircraft fire. The first two loads hit south of the camp and a third load hit both in the camp and just off the south wall. One drop landed in the minefields.

I was the closest to that one, so I took two indigenous personnel into the minefield to retrieve what we could. One of the indigenous soldiers was killed outright and the other was wounded badly. I picked him up on my back—he weighed about, at the most, one hundred pounds—and I carried him back into the compound. Well, the NVA soldiers were having fun with this. They shot him on my back. When I got him back in the camp he was dead, and they had also wounded me a little through his body.

I went back into the minefield, though, and got some ammunition and took it back to my mortar position. Then I decided to go back after some water they had dropped in—with the water tower out of commission I knew we would need it. The water was in those metal military cans, and I had one in each hand when NVA soldiers had some more fun with me. They shot at the cans instead of me. When I got back into the camp there was very little water in them, just a little bit in the bottom. They had shot both cans full of holes.

While I was doing this, Wayne Murray was with Jimmy Taylor and the two of them took aim at the NVA who were shooting at me. "We would kinda pop up and they would shoot at us. Jimmy Taylor, who had a thirty-aught-six rifle with a scope on it, would shoot them. I think he killed twelve or thirteen of them or knocked them down for sure," Murray said.

Every little bit of resupply helped because we desperately needed it, especially the ammunition. But bringing in resupplies was tough for the pilots because they had to deal with both enemy fire and also fire from our own troops. Several members of the 141 Company were seen firing on resupply aircraft as they flew over the camp. This was not "friendly" fire they might have done accidentally. It was treachery.

An American, I'm not sure who, apprehended two of the 141 irregulars and brought them at gunpoint to Blair, who turned them over to Dung, the LLDB camp commander, recommending they be executed for their treachery. Dung, though, refused and said the men were loyal, so all we could do was report this situation to the higher-ups. We did put some Nungs on them to keep a close watch, and the fate of those two CIDG irregulars is unknown, though they were likely killed by the Nungs.

At about six o'clock a Marine CH-34 Seahorse helicopter from Thailand attempted to land in the camp to evacuate the wounded, but it was downed by enemy fire. A few minutes later, another CH-34 helicopter dropped in amid a hail of enemy small-arms fire and successfully evacuated twenty-six wounded men, including John Bradford, and the four uninjured crew members of the first downed Seahorse.

When I was putting Bradford on the plane, the indigenous soldiers were mobbing the helicopter. "They were hanging all over that son of a gun," Bradford said. "The pilot got it up and had to shake the helicopter to get them off. It was a mob scene."

I know at least one of those men trying to stow away was shot and killed by a North Vietnamese soldier, and the aircraft got out of there safely.

That night, we knew the enemy was probably getting ready for an all-out onslaught the next day, and all we could do was try to hold it together until the weather broke and maybe help could come. From about eight till midnight, the camp was hit with several mortar rounds, but it was generally quiet. We were alone except for a single AC-47 flare gunship that stayed on station all night, flying at about a thousand feet above the thick cloud cover. It couldn't do much for us, but it was comforting to hear the engine droning overhead and to speak to the pilot.

CHAPTER TEN

ANOTHER DAY OF PERDITION

SOMETIME AROUND TWO OR THREE in the morning on March 10, the NVA opened up with everything they had. The inside of the camp was engulfed in flames and it seemed like one continuous explosion. We were receiving intense and accurate mortar fire, antitank rockets, and machine gun, recoilless rifle, and rifle gunfire. It was ferocious. By five o'clock, all of the bunkers on the camp's walls had been destroyed and most of our mortars were out of commission. That's when the NVA began attacking the camp's south and east walls with waves and waves of men.

As they began sending in attack forces, I noticed that there was a pattern to it. The North Vietnamese would assemble in their foxholes and start chanting, then they would send a large amount of mortar fire in on us. When that fire lifted, the ground troops would move forward in a mass assault underneath the fire.

We were able to stop them two or three times, and about that time I noticed one of the North Vietnamese commanders would pop off a little green star cluster illumination round just before they attacked. I figured out this was the signal for the enemy's men to move in and I thought, "Maybe we can stop this easy."

The next time the mortars and artillery barrage came in, I popped off a little green star cluster I had. They took the bait and assaulted right into their own fire. I eliminated a company of them with their help, so they changed signals. No more green stars from the NVA after that.

At this point we were having to do almost hand-to-hand combat with the enemy, and most of them appeared to be NVA soldiers, not Viet Cong, because they were dressed in neat, clean khaki-green uniforms and they were very well equipped, too. Very few of them wore tiger-stripe or other camouflage or pajamalike uniforms. This was a professional army. And there were a lot of them.

Carnahan, however, had an encounter that showed more than the NVA were involved.

He said he was looking toward the south when he saw a red star cluster go off, then "all heck busted loose." A little later he heard the south wall had been breached, and he was headed along the south wall trench with Sam Carter when they saw five men walking toward them.

"I asked Captain Carter if they weren't Viet Cong and he said they were his people [Nungs]," Carnahan recalled. "I asked him if he was sure and he said yes, but called one of the interpreters over to make sure."

Though the interpreter agreed the men were Nungs, and they were dressed like Nungs in jungle camouflage, Carnahan noticed something about them. "They had bushes and limbs stuck down between their clothing and the web gear," he said. They were Viet Cong.

In addition to NVA and VC, there were some other forces fighting us, too. I can't recall exactly when this happened, but I do know I saw at least one of the enemy wearing a Chinese uniform. He was standing there surveying the situation and I shot at him, but I missed.

Victor Underwood recalled seeing another kind of soldier there, too. "There was this one big guy I shot," Underwood said. "He had round eyes and black hair on his arms, which the Vietnamese did not. He was wearing a silver belt buckle with a red star on it and had a silver thing on his hat with a red star, too. He could have been a Russian or a Frenchman."

As the enemy came into camp, I do know our men on the south wall and from the northern part of the east wall kept pushing them back, but when one wave was shot down, another would come in. They all tried very hard to keep the enemy out, but the area held by the 141 Company, however, was a different story. Not only did the 141 fail to resist the enemy, but a number of them actually helped the enemy over the wall and into the camp, and many began fighting with the NVA, turning on the rest of us in the camp.

While a lot of this was going on, I was in my mortar pit, which at that point was still operating, even though the indigenous troops helping me in the pit and I had been blown from it three times. At one point when I was in the pit even our cook was in there helping me, but he was killed in one of the explosions.

Sometime in that time frame, the NVA decided to start a hand grenade fight. The first few they sent our way were either short or long over the pit, but they finally got one in with us, and one of my indigenous mortar crew members tried to play soccer with it and kick it into the grenade sump, where it would do less damage. He lost a leg and I got some shrapnel out of it.

They were using Chinese hand grenades, which had handles on them, and I was fortunate enough to catch one. I guess that was another time my high school sports background came in handy—I had been a catcher on the Waurika baseball team. I sent it right back at them and got an airburst right above where it came from. The NVA lost interest in the grenade fighting for a while then.

Throughout it all, we kept the mortar operating by taking wood from the empty mortar-round boxes and using that to reinforce the mortar's bipods, to make it substantial enough that we could continue firing. Other than that, we were down to using small arms—rifles and pistols. My sawed-off shotgun I had modified for jungle fighting came in handy more than once during this part of the battle.

It was on the morning of the tenth, about six o'clock, that US air strikes were delivered immediately north and south of the camp and, though the ground fog was heavy, the cloud ceiling had lifted enough to let some navy Douglas A-1E Skyraiders, single-seat attack aircraft, come through. One of the navy fighters off board ship broke through the cloud cover someway, and he asked me where I wanted him to put some ordinance. I told him to put it on the south wall. He said, "Right on the wall?"

"That's correct," I said. "We don't hold that south wall anymore."

But I also told him, "When you come in on that wall and drop your ordinance, you're going to have to pull right as hard as you can." There was a mountain straight ahead.

He did exactly what I asked him to do except pull right, and he fire-balled into the mountain. That really bothered me. Someway he didn't follow my instructions or maybe I shouldn't have put him in that situation. He didn't make it.

We began placing fire on the defenders of the south and east walls, and the remainder of the Nung platoon and the civilians in the reserve force went to the center of the camp and tried to counterattack, but they could not keep the enemy from coming in. After suffering major casualties, though, the NVA had to pull back to the western portion of the camp and the north wall.

A while later, the enemy put some RPGs (rocket propelled grenades) right onto my position and killed my mortar crew, again. It blew the pit to pieces, too, so that it was all but collapsed. I had to make a run for the commo bunker, which was only a few feet away, and they assaulted us real heavy as I ran. McCann, Pointon, an interpreter, and I took cover, but for some reason McCann stood straight up and he was killed instantly. Pointon was hiding behind a fifty-five-gallon barrel used to bring in fuel for the generator, when he got hit with what I believe was three rounds through the chest and a round in each arm.

Later Pointon remembered he felt like someone had hit him in the chest with a baseball bat. We got him in the commo bunker and I bandaged him up as well as I could, wrapping his whole upper body in bandages. Pointon said the doctor who worked on him after he was evacuated told him that wrapping was the best bandaging he had ever seen.

I also gave Pointon a heavy dose of morphine for the pain. I had a little packet of morphine syrettes that had probably six ampoules of morphine in it, and I think I gave them all to him. Because his upper body was so damaged there was no place to put in a blood expander, so I cut into his foot and then his leg with a rusty TL-29 lineman tool pocketknife, which we used for everything so it was not too sanitary, and gave him some blood expander that way. It worked pretty well.

Even though the mortar pit was destroyed, there was still some ammunition there, so Wayne Murray and I left the commo bunker and went back after it. But when we got there, an NVA soldier jumped right on Murray's back. He wanted an American prisoner. But he failed because I was able to get the NVA soldier off Murray.

While all of this was going on, the rest of the Americans were fighting their own battles. After the NVA had occupied the entire south wall, Vic Underwood along with Carnahan and Carter were there and, using M-79s and M-16s, they killed a lot of the NVA soldiers. Underwood later said the enemy, once inside the camp, didn't seem to know what they were supposed to do next, and they would stand up and look around. As he said, they made good targets.

Another time during the battle, when I was manning the mortar pit, Mari was over in the northwest bunker with

Jimmy Taylor where a company was charging him, and he wanted some mortar fire on them. He said bring it in close. Then closer. Finally he said, "Now fire for effect."

I don't know whether I had a bad round or failed to pull the safety on one, but Mari said a mortar round hit the leader of the NVA company in the head and didn't go off. It killed him just by hitting him without exploding.

I told Mari later, "There's nothing to that. We don't even have to use explosives, just let me know where you want it." Of course, there is no way I could have done that again.

As the fighting continued that morning, Murray and Phil Stahl were in a trench together and were taking mortar rounds when the South Vietnamese soldier who was manning a machine gun with them cut and ran.

Stahl had actually been tagged earlier in the battle for medevac because of a hand wound, but Blair had asked him to stay. "As that chopper was coming in, I said 'Look, Stahl, you've got your ticket out and you can certainly go, but if you go I've only got Carnahan left as a medic and this battle is just getting under way,'" Blair recalled. "He said, 'Sure, sir, I'll stay.'"

It was a fateful decision.

"I told Phil to get the machine gun and put some firepower out there because you could see them. They were coming in through the wire," Murray said. "Phil went over to the machine gun and I think he fired about a belt before all of a sudden there was an explosion. I got hit in the hand, arm, and leg with shrapnel and my M-16 was hit right where the magazine goes in, so it became nonfunctional. I'm sitting there yelling, 'Medic!' and then I realized that was stupid because the medic,

Stahl, was down where the explosion occurred. I went down and he was pretty badly destroyed."

From ten o'clock to noon, those pilots bombed and strafed the camp, and they inflicted heavy casualties on the enemy, enough to keep them out of the little ground we still held. But they were risking a lot to be there for us, a reality that soon played out.

CHAPTER ELEVEN

VALOR ON THE GROUND; FROM THE SKIES

DURING THE MORNING of March 10, the clouds lifted enough to let air support come in. At about ten o'clock, Blair recommended that B-52 bombers conduct heavy arc light bombings just south of the camp in the Be Loung Valley and along the ridgelines east and west of the camp. Unfortunately, the higher-ups disapproved that request, though they did approve dropping bombs and napalm and fire rockets.

Just before noon on March 10, Underwood came to me and let me know that one of the Skyraider fighter planes had crash-landed on the airstrip and the pilot, who we later found out was Major Stafford ("Jump") Myers, had gotten out and run to a berm east of the runway. Myers was under heavy fire from enemy riflemen and machine gunners located east of the airstrip, and our soldiers in the northeast apex of the bunker were returning fire on them, trying to keep the enemy from maneuvering in on Myers.

Underwood told me he was taking five Nungs outside the camp to retrieve Myers, and he and his group headed out to try and get the pilot inside the camp, but when they got through the main gate they were pinned down. All five were killed and Vic had to take cover in a shallow hole and couldn't move. Then another air force Skyraider came in with his wheels down.

Blair described the plane as it came in, saying it descended from the south to the north of the strip with its landing gear down. Those in the camp seeing this thought it was crashing, but they were wrong. US Air Force Major Bernie Fisher, the pilot of that plane, had seen Myers go down and assumed his fellow pilot was probably injured and in danger of being captured, so he called in and said he was going in after him.

Fisher landed and taxied to the end of the airstrip where he turned around and pulled up by Myers, who jumped into the cockpit headfirst, and they took off with a lot of NVA shooting at them. Fisher's plane was struck with nineteen bullets, but he still managed to get his aircraft off the ground and out of there.

Underwood said later he recalled thinking as he watched Fisher descend to the airstrip, "Oh shit! Not another one." But instead of crashing, Underwood watched him take back off with Myers's legs hanging out of the plane. In the process, Fisher also helped Underwood, who was able to run into camp while the NVA were shooting at Fisher. This act not only earned Major Bernie Fisher the first US Air Force Medal of Honor, Underwood said it "saved my ass."

Not long after that happened, at about noon, a radio transmission went out to higher headquarters from Hoover, or maybe Blair, saying "Need reinforcements, without them kiss us goodbye."

We kept telling higher headquarters we could not receive resupply without getting reinforcements first. But about that time a CV-2 Caribou attempted another resupply drop that landed about sixty-five feet west of the western apex bunker, and the enemy shot it all to pieces. We didn't get a bit of that one.

A message came through about twelve forty-five that afternoon from higher-ups saying, "Green Berets, by God we're trying," but there was still no word about whether we would get reinforcements.

Wayne Murray recalled a radio message we got telling us there would be no reinforcements and he said it went something like this: "The Marine Corps cannot come out and reinforce you. Remember, God and the Green Berets are with you." Wayne remembered thinking, "You know, I'd rather have the Marine Corps."

Wayne said, "It was frustrating to me because not more than three weeks before the battle, General Lewis Walt, commander of Marine Amphibious Force and 3rd Marine Division in Vietnam, had been at our camp and said, 'You hold them off for twenty-four hours and we will have a battalion of Marines out here.' Well, we held them off for thirty-eight hours. The Marines never came."

Dave Blair, who admitted he was not happy about the lack of support from the Marines, later said he understood the decision. "General Walt treated us Special Forces just like we were his own Marines," Blair said. "But at the time they didn't have the troops available for a major battle and we had an NVA division that was investing just on us. It would have been jumping into the hornet's nest."

By now we realized if reinforcements were coming at all, they wouldn't be there soon enough, and our ammunition was almost exhausted, so we decided we had to at least take back the western half of the camp in order to hold up our defenses for the night and keep enough of the camp open for us to receive future ammunition resupply drops.

We had tried a number of counterattacks that morning as the NVA were swarming into the camp at the south wall, with the help of the 141 Company, because we knew we had to do something to reclaim some ground inside the camp. The Nungs' commanding officer led one assault and they did retake the eastern portion of the camp, and we tried to get Dung to help us retake part of the south wall. He just hid in his bunker.

Underwood, Blair, Carnahan, Carter, and I attempted to move some of the enemy out ourselves. Armed with hand grenades and M-16s, we started across the camp toward the south wall, throwing hand grenades at any enemy we could see. This attempt might have been successful had the CIDG irregulars or the LLDB men helped, but they didn't. Most of them cowered in the north wall trench for much of the rest of the battle.

Dave Blair recalled that the decision to launch another counterattack that afternoon was made so we could hold out for just one more night. "We didn't really intend to give up the camp and we didn't expect to be evacuated," he said. "But our idea was, if we could reestablish a perimeter, maybe we could get through the night and maybe there would be enough space there to get an airdrop in the next day."

A little before two in the afternoon we called in on the radio saying, "Want strikes on south wall, inside fifty meters on east side of runway, and on east wall. US attempting to assault from north and south and to sweep the south wall."

The air strikes came in and our counterattack began at 2:10 P.M. My group, which included Mari, Robbins, and Murray, ran out of the commo bunker and to my mortar pit.

None of us got any farther; the enemy assault was just too strong for our limited number of men to combat. But we did give them something to think about. Dave Blair later described it by saying that the enemy "went limping back over to the north wall, and they looked like chickens whose feathers had been ruffled."

During that counterattack, Underwood and Carnahan had gotten about halfway across the camp near the commo bunker when they had to take cover behind a Conex container with Underwood on one side and Carnahan on the other. According to Underwood, an NVA soldier threw a hand grenade, wounding them both, and then Underwood jumped around Carnahan and saw the man who had thrown the grenade running back toward the south wall. Underwood threw his last hand grenade at the NVA and hit him in the back, blowing him all to pieces. They then pulled back to the north wall and Carnahan, who had a broken leg, took care of their wounds.

After the failed counterattacks, we only had the north wall and the commo bunker in our control and all we could do was try to bomb them out of place, so we called in a strike on the entire camp, except for the north wall and the commo bunker.

During the counterattack, Blair got lucky. Before he was killed, Stahl, who had lived through a previous attack at another camp and was "the voice of doom" at A Shau, had dug a little trench or foxhole. "I was mad at him and said, 'Stahl, calm down, we're going to hold,'" Blair recalled. Stahl never got to use that foxhole, but Blair did. "As we went out to do the counterattack, I got into this little hole he had dug and I appreciated it."

Blair also recalled how luck worked in that battle. According to Blair, during the counterattack he was assaulting out across the area and throwing grenades and shooting as they tried to reestablish a perimeter to get through the night.

"There was an old M72 LAW light antitank weapon lying around and in all the shelling, fragments had penetrated its fiberglass tube and I didn't know if it was any good or not, but we were getting pretty desperate," he said. "I pulled it up and cocked it but it had all these holes in it. God looks out for idiots, I guess, but I tried to fire it and I knew I was going to get hurt because of the holes in the rocket."

"Well, fortunately the thing didn't fire," he continued. "I recocked it three times and it wouldn't fire, so I sort of threw it in their direction and crawled back. But, you know, it would have killed me if it had fired. I didn't think about it at the time. All I was thinking was 'Get those people.' But sometimes you're just lucky."

That was not the only time that Blair got lucky. "At some point I was crawling and walking down a trench, stumbling over the poor old wounded people lying everywhere, and trying to check on Carnahan and Underwood. When I got close, Carnahan or Underwood, I'm not sure which, told me to watch out, that a sniper was shooting at everyone who went across a trench. I started to hop across and that guy shot at me, but apparently hit my grenade. There was a big puff of white smoke and fragments stinging me. Carnahan and Underwood were right there and I said, "God damn, what are they doing, shooting explosive bullets?'

"Carnahan said, 'My God, sir . . .'"

The fuse assembly from the hand grenade was hanging down from Blair's pouch. "The bullet would have gone right into my gut if it hadn't hit that grenade," he said, "and it didn't detonate the blasting cap, otherwise the bullet wound or the grenade would have killed me and them, too."

At some point that afternoon, we noticed a battalion-sized enemy contingent was forming on the east side of the airstrip, apparently preparing for an assault, and we called in for an immediate air strike. Two B-57 Canberra bombers each made single low-altitude bombing runs with antipersonnel bombs, catching the enemy just as they dashed across the airstrip. That particular NVA battalion was almost completely destroyed, and thanks to the bombing we were able to keep them from reaching the east wall.

After our failed counterattack, we all gathered in the north wall and commo bunker area where we redistributed ammunition and tried to restore some order within our badly battered ranks. At that point there were bodies everywhere, including those choking the north wall, and about half the garrison was dead or badly wounded. All of us were at least somewhat wounded. We had enough ammunition for each man who was still battle-able to have about twenty rounds of ammo, and among us we had twelve M26 hand grenades.

All we could do was wait for reinforcements and hope we could hold on long enough for those to arrive. As we waited, the camp continued to be pounded by heavy explosions from what we later learned may have been 120 mm mortars, several of which were near hits scored on the commo bunker. The enemy kept bombarding us with mortars, and NVA riflemen and machine gunners continued to fire on us from within the camp.

At this point, an interpreter overheard some of the LLDB regulars and CIDG irregulars discussing the possibility of surrendering to the enemy. Blair told them there would be no surrender. We and the Nungs planned to hold the north wall at all costs. We had almost no ammunition, our casualties were extreme, we were hungry and thirsty, and many of our men were demoralized, but at 4:30 P.M. we were still fighting, and most of us were determined to fight to the finish.

That's when a call came in from higher headquarters to evacuate the camp. The fighting instinct was still strong in us, but we had no choice. It was a direct order from Lieutenant Colonel Kenneth Bradford Facey. They didn't ask us if we wanted to go, but I can tell you that if we had not gone, there would be no one left alive to tell the story from the US side.

"When they told me to prepare for evacuation, I objected," recalled Blair. "I didn't want to quit. If you're a combat soldier, you just don't want to get whipped, plus, we were killing a bunch of them.

"I kept saying, 'Hey, rather than trying to get us out, send in reinforcements. I think anything will be effective.' I didn't want to quit the fight. In fact, when they told me to break out I said, 'Put an arc light down and chances are you'll miss us.'"

"We were killers," he continued. "That's all you can say, and I think it became an obsession for many of us—to kill as many of them as we could—because I don't think any of us thought we were going to live through it, and you get over being scared and you're just fighting."

But Blair later said the decision to evacuate was the right decision, despite how the actual evacuation went.

CHAPTER TWELVE

GIVING UP THE GHOST

A T 3:00 P.M., the Marines committed sixteen to eighteen helicopters to evacuate all of us still alive in Camp A Shau. The mission went to the HMM-163, a Marine helicopter squadron at Phu Bai nicknamed the "Ridge Runners" that became famous for their many rescues and assault support flights during the Vietnam War. We were notified at 4:30 P.M. that the survivors would be evacuated from a landing zone a few hundred yards north of the camp.

We immediately began destroying all the communications equipment and classified documents in the American communications bunker, especially any documents that might give information to the NVA about our plans or the intel we had gathered. We didn't want anything to fall into their hands, so we burned it all. Hoover piled all the communications equipment up in the commo bunker, and just before he left the bunker he set it on fire with five incendiary grenades.

The LLDB commander and the CIDG and Nung leaders were filled in about the plan for withdrawal, which was that, when the helicopters began to approach, Carter and Blair would take down the wire barricades on the path leading from the north wall side gate. Underwood and Carnahan and a squad of the Nungs from the Mike Force would spearhead the breakout and lead the way to the landing zone, where they were supposed to help organize the evacuation.

While that was happening, the able-bodied Americans and Nungs were to stay behind in the camp to cover the withdrawal while the able-bodied CIDG irregulars were to help all the wounded down to the landing areas and get them on the helicopters. The wounded were to be the first priority for evacuation, then the men in the landing zone, followed by the rear guard. According to Blair, the information about this plan was definitely passed on to the CIDG troops, based on the ripple of conversation along the trench.

At 5:20 P.M. we heard the sound of the helicopters approaching from the north, and they found a little hole in the clouds to drop in. Blair said later, "It looked like a witches' scene from Macbeth . . . the fog was beginning to swirl and the cloud ceiling above the camp was dropping fast."

Fog and clouds gave the helicopters, and their accompanying HU-1B "Huey" gunships that provided aerial cover for the extraction, some cover as they came in. But as they approached, the enemy began an onslaught of rifle, machine gun, and recoilless rifle fire and hit several of the helicopters, crashing two of them. Only half of them were able to land and the remaining ones were waved off.

By this time, at least part of the withdrawal mission had gone as planned. Carter and Blair had crawled out and opened the wire barricades on the path a few minutes before the helicopters arrived, and everyone was set to get on the choppers. But when the CIDG and LLDB men, including the LLDB commander, Dung, saw half the helicopters turn away and Underwood, Carnahan, and their Nungs head toward the landing zone, they rushed out of the camp.

According to Underwood, "They lost control and swarmed out of the camp in a mob. They ran past us, separating me and Carnahan from the Nungs. I tried to shoot Dung, the camp commander, but someone kept getting in my way—lucky for him."

As they ran, many of the South Vietnamese dropped their weapons and also left the wounded behind. Because only about half of the helicopters were able to land, there were too few of them to handle the panicked men, who were fighting one another to get on the choppers, and the helicopters became so overloaded they couldn't take off.

Lieutenant Colonel C. A. "Chuck" House, the US Marine Corps 163rd HMM squadron commander, was flying one of those helicopters and was in the middle of the action. When House saw what was happening, he apparently told his men that if they were overloaded and couldn't kick the men off, they were to shoot them off, an order that later led to House being threatened with court-martial.

House's own helicopter was being mobbed, and when they finally got enough people off its runners to lift up about ten feet from the ground, their tail rotor was shot. The chopper came crashing down.

In the middle of all this the rearguard, which I was part of, was leapfrogging to get everyone out, but about this time the NVA infantrymen in the camp renewed their assaults, and the rearguard action became extremely violent. We managed to hold the north wall until everyone still alive was out, though, or so we thought.

Dave Blair said he saw none of this because he and Sam Carter, along with six of Carter's Nungs, had stayed behind in the camp as a covering and holding force, trying to contain the enemy while the rest of the camp made it to the landing zone. As the rearguard moved toward the helicopters, picking up wounded men who had fallen in the landing zone area on the way, I ran into Mari, who said Jimmy Taylor, who was severely wounded, was still in the camp in the northwestern corner bunker near the airstrip. We had to go back in the camp to get him.

To get to him, we had to follow a trench that led to the bunker, and just as we were going down the trench, an enemy soldier jumped into the ditch a few feet from me. He had his weapon up. Mine was slung by my side. I pulled it up as he shot, and just by luck his bullet hit my magazine and stuck there. It cooked off a couple of rounds, but I was fortunate enough to have a round in the magazine, and I shot him in the eye. He threw his weapon down and ran. I didn't pursue him. I just kept going toward the bunker.

We got Taylor on a stretcher and ran back down the trench with him to the side gate, where we had to fight our way out again. When we got there, all of the helicopters were gone except for the wreckage of the two that had been shot down. There was no ride out.

During this time Underwood, who was badly wounded in the legs and had been trampled by the panicked CIDG and LLDB soldiers as they rushed the helicopters, had witnessed House's bird crash. "House came over to me and said, 'I've got a map and you've got a compass. Let's get out of here.'"

Vic and House were separated in all the confusion, so Underwood began looking for other Americans. That's when he heard someone yell, "Sergeant Underwood, get me out of here."

"It was George Pointon and he was bandaged up and looked like a mummy, but he was mobile," recalled Underwood.

Pointon had been in the commo bunker at the time of the evacuation. He said someone tried to put him on a stretcher, but he told them he would walk out because there was no way they would get him out on a stretcher through the wire barrier.

According to Pointon, someone told him to follow a path that had been cut through the wire toward a landing zone, and he recalled staggering along by himself with an IV bottle attached to his body and all bandaged up. Somehow he became separated from the other guys, so he kept going out and made it through the wire, then he headed north through the elephant grass and found his way to the creek that ran near the camp.

"I got to the creek and I knew it ran east to west, and I thought I could walk down the creek and maybe intercept the other guys," he said. "As I walked along, I looked up and who do I see but Bao, my main guy on the CIDG team. He was sitting on the edge of the creek leaning on a tree. He had taken a round through the leg and couldn't walk. I stopped and I was going to stay with him but he said no. He reached in a pocket, though, and handed me a letter. Then he said, 'Take the letter and give it to my family.' I realized that he had figured out the only way he was not going to die is if I lived."

When Pointon found Underwood, a Marine gunship was still flying fairly low in the area and they were able to flag it down. "The door gunner and I helped George onto the aircraft and I started to get in, too," Underwood said. But then someone on the aircraft pulled a pistol out and pointed it right at Underwood. He sidestepped and realized what they were doing. "They shot a South Vietnamese soldier off my back," Underwood said. "The helicopters took off and left me standing there."

Pointon remembered a big Marine jumped off the helicopter to help him on but once Pointon was in the chopper, the CIDG soldiers started mobbing it, so the Marine literally began throwing them off. "He finally pulled out his .45 and started shooting them off," Pointon said.

Sometime during all of this, another Marine gunship spotted Wayne Murray, who had been severely injured. They dropped their pods, landed, the crew chief got off the helicopter and helped Murray in, and they took off.

Though the Marines had managed to evacuate more than seventy men, including four LLDB soldiers (only one of which we later discovered was actually wounded) and four wounded Americans—Carnahan, Pointon, Robbins, and Murray—there were still more than one hundred of us left behind: seven Special Forces men, eight crew members from the downed helicopters, about ninety of our CIDG and LLDB men, and two civilians.

It was time to evade rather than evacuate.

CHAPTER THIRTEEN

LAST MEN STANDING

REALIZING OUR ONLY HOPE of survival was to evade the enemy until help could come, the USASF soldiers still on the ground with the main group began trying to organize the survivors.

Everyone was in a state of shock and demoralized at having been left behind. According to Blair, some of the CIDG men literally lay or squatted in fetal positions and were wailing. One of the downed CH-34 helicopters was crammed full of wounded CIDG men who, Blair remembered, refused to get out and join the evaders. They literally had to be kicked, beaten, and rough-handled to force them on their feet and into a file formation for the evasion.

Blair also remembered being so thirsty when he came out of the camp that he drank water from a mud puddle, not the stream, which later proved to be a problem for him.

During this time, Blair and Carter located House, the senior combat arms officer present, and told him the USASF men would follow his orders, but they were preparing to evade the enemy with the hope rescue helicopters could pick them up the following day. If help did not come, the plan was to infiltrate through enemy-held territory toward Hue.

According to Blair and Underwood, House was sure no further rescue attempts would be made because of the high degree of risk involved, and he wanted to evade toward Thailand, several days' walk away.

At that point everyone was exhausted and wounded. Blair said some of the men who had been burned from the helicopter crash had skin hanging off them and some were screaming; others were on litters or simply limping along. They were all in bad shape.

Blair recalled the exchange on that decision. "I said, 'Sir, you have to be kidding. Look at us. We can't go that far. We're going to have to move toward Hue and we'll be lucky if we make it there.'

"House was furious and he was threatening me and Mari with court-martial when I said to him, 'Look, Colonel, I don't care where you go but I'm going to Hue.'"

According to Blair, that conversation only took a few seconds. By 5:45 P.M. the evaders were moving west toward Laos with five USASF soldiers interspersed throughout the file to control and provide security for the wounded men. House and the other seven Marines were close to the front of the formation.

They kept moving through the night, stopping to rest when they could and realizing they didn't have all the men.

"When I was walking tail gunner after daylight," said Underwood, "one of the Nungs said, 'VC come. VC come.' We put together a hasty ambush and here comes a Nung, and right behind him comes ol' Minter Hoover. Hoover was about as white as a sheet. He was one scared boy. I jumped out of the brush and grabbed him and I thought he was going to have a heart attack, but he was happy to get back with the rest of us."

Sometime that morning, using a signal mirror and a smoke grenade, they got the attention of an aircraft flying overhead. Using a little H1 radio, they were able to give their coordinates, and two Marine helicopters came in and without landing took House and his crew, Underwood, and the two civilians on board.

"Basically the reason any of us got out of there was a guy named Clark who was a C Detachment commo sergeant," said Underwood. "He took all the frequencies that were assigned to A Shau and got in a plane and started flying the valley listening to all these radios. When the airplane went by, Blair or Mari started calling it and that's how they found us."

That left Blair, Mari, and Hoover still on the ground with about twenty CIDG soldiers, but the next day they were able to signal another aircraft with a mirror, and two helicopters were sent in to get them out. They wouldn't land either, and were dropping strings.

"I told Lew to go up first," recalled Blair. "He said, 'No, you go.' They lowered the penetrator and I went up first to plead with them to send more choppers, and while I was up there, and when they were trying to get people in the harnesses, somebody threw a grenade—I'm not sure if it was one of our own troops, but I suspect it was—and then the shooting started all over the place. We were hovering there, and the other helicopter was moving in with his sling down and I was yelling at Mari and Hoover to 'Get on, get on.'"

"Both of them grabbed on and the pilot took off dragging them through the trees," Blair continued. "Fortunately, it didn't break the cable and they hung on, but only the three of us got out. Honestly, we tried our darnedest to get the others out."

While all of this was going on, I was in another part of the jungle with Sam Carter and some Nungs.

When Mari and I came out of camp with Taylor, there were people yelling, guns were firing, and hand grenades were flying. We were being fired on by the enemy, but much of the fighting was happening among our own troops, who were killing and wounding one another in the chaos of the moment. It smelled like cordite and blood.

In the middle of all that confusion, Mari and I got separated but I ran into Sam Carter, who had five or six Nungs with him. Carter was in horribly bad shape from the building falling on him the first morning of the attack and from all the fighting. He couldn't hear and he was very irrational—he was barely lucid—so I took him and the soldiers, and we carried Jimmy Taylor into the jungle toward higher ground, away from the fighting and toward the Laotian border. In about an hour, though, Taylor died and all we could do was cache his body.

There were many decisions to be made at that moment, but the toughest was the decision to leave Taylor behind. It was a necessary decision, though, because there was nothing else we could do for him, and trying to carry his body through that thick jungle might well have meant we all would die. I thought that, having recorded the coordinates of where we left him, we would be able to return and get him later.

Bennie G. Adkins and Mary Arington were married on April 7, 1956, in her family's living room near Opelika, Alabama. At the time Bennie was an army sergeant assigned to Fort Benning, Georgia, and Mary was working in a local sewing factory and had met Bennie through one of her girlfriends who was dating another Fort Benning soldier. (Author's collection)

After his first tour in Vietnam in 1963, Bennie returned to his home base in Fort Bragg, North Carolina, where he was awarded his first Purple Heart for a punji stick injury he sustained during that tour. (Author's collection)

Bennie, a native of Oklahoma, Mary, and their children went home to visit his large, closely knit family as often as possible. This photo was taken in his parents' house in Waurika during a visit between his first and second tours in Vietnam, and before the Battle of A Shau. Their son, Keith, is peeking around his father. (Author's collection)

This photo of Adkins was taken during his first tour in Vietnam and was likely the photo used on wanted posters distributed by the North Vietnamese and their sympathizers as they sought Bennie for his actions against them during the Battle of A Shau and later when he was part of the Studies and Observation Group. (Author's collection)

Because of the language barriers and lack of technical supplies and knowledge to teach the troops, Special Forces soldiers often resorted to drawing pictures and maps in the soil as they trained the troops. (Victor Underwood's collection)

The Civilian Irregular Defense Group (CIDG) force included men committed to the cause of freeing their country from the incoming waves of North Vietnamese and the in-country Viet Cong; forces also often included infiltrators working with the North Vietnamese and Viet Cong. (Victor Underwood's collection)

In Vietnam, Special Forces troops were primarily teachers working with the CIDG forces to train them in protecting their villages and their country. Language barriers were often a problem for the Americans and the troops were often young, inexperienced men who had a lot to learn. (Victor Underwood's collection)

Before the March 1966 battle there, Camp A Shau was a remote, understaffed, and undersupplied fort surrounded by mountains and jungle in South Vietnam's Northern Highlands region. The triangular design of the camp was typical of many CIDG training camps throughout the country during the Vietnam War. (Davis Blair's collection)

This 81 mm mortar pit just outside the Special Forces team house at Camp A Shau was little more than a shallow hole dug into the ground and reinforced with sandbags. This pit, which was Adkins's assigned position for the battle, was a main target of enemy mortar fire during the battle and was hit at least three times with such force that it blew Adkins and his crew out of the pit, yet Adkins continued to fire the mortar until late in the battle with remarkable accuracy. (Davis Blair's collection)

Sergeant First Class Victor Underwood was a member of the A-503 Mike Force team that came into the camp March 7 to provide security while the camp was being reinforced in preparation for the battle. (Victor Underwood's collection)

Captain Sam Carter, leader of the Mike Force team, was asleep in the supply room when the first round of mortars came in early on March 9 and collapsed the building on him. It took him several hours to dig himself out of the rubble before he could join the others in the fighting. (Victor Underwood's collection)

Sergeant John Bradford came into A Shau as a member of the Mike Force two days before the battle began. Though he was injured early in the battle, the scoped rifle Bradford had brought with him to A Shau came in handy later for Victor Underwood, who used it to pick off a number of the enemy. (Victor Underwood's collection)

This photo of the original A-503 Mike Force team included several men who fought at A Shau, including Sergeant Minter Hoover (front row, fourth from the left), Staff Sergeant and medic Billie Hall and Sergeant First Class Victor Underwood (back row, third and fourth from the left, respectively) and Captain Tennis "Sam" Carter (back row, far right). (Victor Underwood's collection)

Lodging for the soldiers when in-country varied from camp to camp, and this was "home sweet home" for Davis Blair at another camp in Vietnam. While Blair did keep photos of his family while in-country, Bennie did not because he feared that the enemy might find a way to use those photos to identify him. (Davis Blair's collection)

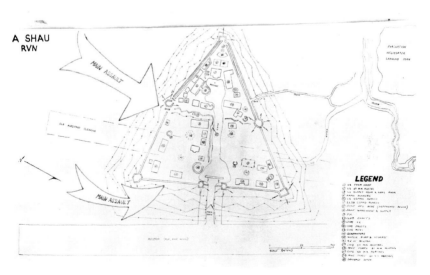

This map, used by Davis Blair in his after-action report, shows the different angles of attack used by the North Vietnamese during the Battle of A Shau. (Davis Blair's collection)

Bennie and his fellow soldiers were honored after the battle with a number of commendations, including the Purple Heart. Bennie is shown here being congratulated by Lieutenant Colonel Kenneth Bradford Facey, the C Team commander during the battle. (Victor Underwood's collection)

CENTER: Several weeks after the Battle of A Shau, the surviving Special Forces soldiers were honored with an array of commendations including Purple Hearts. This photo shows Bennie (center) with A-102 team sergeant Robert Gibson to his left and A-102 senior medic Vernon Carnahan to his right.
BOTTOM: CIDG and LLDB soldiers who fought in the battle were also honored at a ceremony following the battle. This unidentified South Vietnamese soldier receives a commendation from Lieutenant Colonel Kenneth Bradford Facey while, from left, Bennie, Vernon Carnahan, and A Team Specialist Herril Robbins look on. (Victor Underwood's collection)

TOP: Among the Special Forces A-102 men who survived the battle and received Purple Hearts during in-country ceremonies were, *front row from left*: Captain Davis Blair, Lieutenant Lewis A. Mari, and Master Sergeant Robert Gibson. CENTER: Wayne Murray, a demolitions expert, receives congratulations from Lieutenant Colonel Kenneth Bradford Facey. (Victor Underwood's collection)

The survivors of the Battle of A Shau who were honored at a ceremony several weeks after the battle include, from left, Davis Blair, Lewis Mari, Robert Gibson, Bennie, Vernon Carnahan, Herril Robbins, and Wayne Murray. Ken Facey, commander of the C Team that supported the soldiers at A Shau during the battle, is at the podium. (Davis Blair's collection)

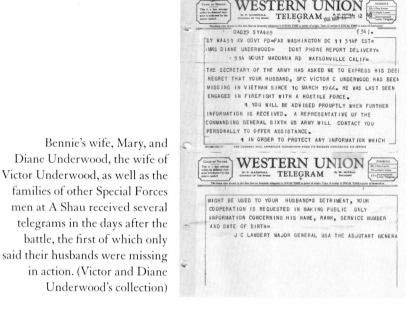

Bennie's wife, Mary, and Diane Underwood, the wife of Victor Underwood, as well as the families of other Special Forces men at A Shau received several telegrams in the days after the battle, the first of which only said their husbands were missing in action. (Victor and Diane Underwood's collection)

Following the Battle of A Shau, the scene at Camp A Shau was one of utter devastation. This aerial shot shows the remains of its buildings and equipment. (Davis Blair's collection)

A small team of Special Forces soldiers, including these two unidentified men carrying a body bag, went back into Camp A Shau on May 14, 1966, to retrieve the bodies of their fellow Special Forces soldiers. The exercise took twenty minutes. (Davis Blair's collection)

LEFT: American and South Vietnamese bodies were strewn throughout the camp two months after the battle when a team of Americans went back to A Shau to retrieve their fallen colleagues and bury the bodies of their South Vietnamese counterparts. BELOW: Bodies littered the camp after the battle and, though the North Vietnamese had come back to the camp to retrieve their dead, the South Vietnamese and American bodies were left to decay. (Davis Blair's collection)

The teams that went in to retrieve the bodies at Camp A Shau included one detail to provide security, one for recovery of the US bodies, and a third to bury indigenous soldiers. That team included A Shau survivors Wayne Murray, Sam Carter, Victor Underwood, and Lewis Mari. (Davis Blair's collection)

The recovery team had to search the entire camp to look for bodies, and many were found under the rubble and litter of the camp, but the body of Jimmy Taylor, which Adkins had cached in the jungle as they evacuated the camp, has never been found. (Davis Blair's collection)

Pictured above are the remains of the water tower at Camp A Shau, which was badly hit during the early hours of the battle. The rubber container that once held water was still intact as the soldiers evacuated the camp, but it, as well as tires and other equipment, was scavenged by the North Vietnamese following the battle. (Davis Blair's collection)

The concrete and pierced steel planking (PSP) that reinforced the camp was blown to pieces by the heavy mortar fire of the North Vietnamese Army. (Davis Blair's collection)

During the Battle of A Shau, the camp was reduced to rubble by the heavy fire of the North Vietnamese Army. (Davis Blair's collection)

This water-filled hole was what remained of one of the camp's mortar pits after the battle. (Davis Blair's collection)

The PSP used to reinforce the trenches was still standing in parts of the camp after the battle, though the carnage was extensive throughout the area. (Davis Blair's collection)

These trenches that ran around the perimeter of the camp are where many men fought and died during the battle. (Davis Blair's collection)

SGT. 1st CLASS BENNIE G. ADKINS

Opelikan Recommended
For Medal Of Honor

LEFT: Bennie G. Adkins was nominated for the Medal of Honor not long after the Battle of A Shau, an honor that he did not receive until almost fifty years later.

BELOW: After his tours in Vietnam and after serving at Fort Huachuca, Arizona, at the US Army Communications Command, Bennie went on to graduate from the United States Army Sergeants Major Academy in El Paso, Texas. Bennie's wife, Mary, and an unidentified officer awarding Bennie his "brass." (Author's collection)

After Vietnam and after earning the rank of command sergeant major, Bennie was assigned to the Panama Canal Zone in 1976, where he was commandant for the NCO academy and also served as the command sergeant major for Fort Sherman until 1978. (Author's collection)

President Barack Obama bestows the Medal of Honor to retired Command Sergeant Major Bennie G. Adkins in the East Room of the White House, September 15, 2014. Adkins distinguished himself in close-combat fighting against enemy forces on March 9 to 12, 1966. At that time, then–Sergeant First Class Adkins was serving as an Intelligence Sergeant with 5th Special Forces Group, 1st Special Forces at Camp "A Shau," in the Republic of Vietnam. During the 38-hour battle and 48 hours of escape and evasion, Adkins fought using mortars, machine guns, recoilless rifles, small arms, and hand grenades, killing an estimated 135 to 175 of the enemy and sustaining eighteen different wounds. (Department of Defense)

Defense Secretary Chuck Hagel presents Medal of Honor recipient retired Army Command Sergeant Major Bennie G. Adkins with the Medal of Honor flag after inducting him into the Hall of Heroes during a ceremony at the Pentagon, September 16, 2014. (Department of Defense)

CHAPTER FOURTEEN

EVADING THE GHOST

ONCE WE CACHED TAYLOR'S BODY, we moved on in a northwest direction headed for the Vietnam-Laos border. I chose that route because I knew the rest of our survivors were in an area where the Puff the Magic Dragon plane had been shot down the day before. There had been a horrible firefight in that area, so I wanted to avoid it.

The other column of men had made it into the jungle and they were managing to evade the NVA, too. Later, Victor Underwood said he thought that was because the NVA were reorganizing their units and taking care of their wounded. "They knew there were a lot of our people who got out, but I don't think they were really worried about it because there was no place for us to go," said Underwood. "They probably figured they were going to police us up sooner or later."

There are different accounts of how many NVA died in that battle. Underwood said the air force estimated we killed around twelve hundred; the army said eight hundred. I have no idea how many it really was, but I do recall hearing that pilots flying over A Shau in the days after the battle said there was "a wall of bodies" in the camp. A Shau Valley sure did earn its name of the "Valley of Death."

We spent the night trying to get as far away from the enemy as we could, but also resting when we could. It was hard work trying to go up that mountain toward Laos, plus you didn't move that much at night unless you absolutely had to, so we didn't make it very far from the camp that night. But the next morning we got serious about getting out of the area.

I had brought a little FM radio out of the camp with me. It was not powerful—you could barely talk to someone across the room with it—and its antenna had been shot off, but I figured I might be able to get it to work. All of that Green Beret training probably helped with that.

What I needed to do was supplement something for the antenna, but I didn't have wire or anything like that to do it, so I stood in a stream and used the water to ground me. Then I took my little old sawed-off shotgun, which I still had with me, and put it barrel-down on the radio where the antenna connection should have been.

Sure enough—and it was almost a miracle that it worked—I was able to communicate with one of the fixed-wing aircraft circling upstairs, and it happened to be another Special Forces soldier that had our frequencies. They said they would send in two helicopters to get us, so we got busy cutting a little landing pad, enough for one of them to land at a time, using our little flexible camp saws to saw down small trees and pile them up.

We cut just enough so one helicopter at a time could hover over us, and we were going to be hot-hoisted out.

As the first helicopter came in, though, the NVA must have heard it, and they came after us. They shot the helicopter down on the pad and two of its crew members were injured. The second helicopter dropped strings and we were able to get the two wounded Marine helicopter crewmen out, but that's all they could take so we were left on the ground, now with two additional Marines in our group.

We got into a little firefight with the NVA that had shot the helicopter down there at the pad, but it was very short. It must have been just a few NVA who had been trying to see what was happening, rather than a large unit. One of our Nungs was killed in the fight, but we were able to get a machine gun and some C rations off the helicopter before we had to go again, the NVA hot on our heels.

By this time it was getting dark and the foggy, drizzly weather was getting worse, so we knew there was no chance another helicopter could come in for us that night. All we could do was keep moving, which we did all night long, working our way as quietly as possible through the jungle and stopping every three or four hours to exchange fire with the NVA who were following us.

Finally, on the second night in the jungle, we found a little area on high ground and settled in, still waiting for extraction.

CHAPTER FIFTEEN

A TIGER'S TALE

W HAT MAKES VIETNAM'S JUNGLE so unique is that at night there is almost no light because of the thick canopy, so what you "see" is really what you hear.

I had spent enough time in the jungle that I knew most of those sounds, usually the noises made by insects, birds, and monkeys. None of those sounds usually bothered me, though I recall Wayne Murray was not so fond of the gibbon monkeys.

"I'd be out on patrol and start going up a hilltop and I'd see these little brown faces staring out at me from a tree," Murray said, "and all [of] a sudden they'd go 'woop, woop, woop' and everybody for ten miles knew that somebody was out there."

Being in the jungle during wartime did make you sensitive to anything that could give away your location, so the gibbons could definitely be a problem. But the sounds that really bothered me were the ones that didn't fit in the jungle, like the metal of a weapon hitting a stick or a rock, or a motor running somewhere far off, or the sound of aircraft overhead.

During our second night in the jungle, I could hear all the usual animals and hear some of those other sounds, including the voices of the NVA who were following us. They knew we were close. They just couldn't find us. And we wanted to keep it that way.

Our group didn't talk among ourselves at that point, except maybe in an occasional whisper. I guess I did sleep on and off during the night because someone said they kicked me a couple of times for snoring, but mostly we were all alert and listening to the sounds around us.

I can't remember when it happened, but at some point on that night we began hearing a new noise. Something was moving through the brush near us, and all I could tell about it was it was large. Then I began to hear a little growl or two, and then I saw the glint of two large eyes in the dark.

It was a tiger.

Now, I had seen all kinds of animals in Vietnam. I'd seen elephants, water buffalo, deer, and other, more dangerous animals, including spitting cobras and other highly poisonous snakes. I knew there were tigers there, too, and I did catch a glimpse of one once as it jumped across a creek.

Wayne Murray said he never actually saw a tiger, but when he was out on patrol one night and they were hunkered down at an ambush site, he heard something moving around in the jungle nearby. "We got up the next morning and there were huge kitty-cat footprints on the trail," he said. "A tiger had walked right through our ambush site."

Dave Blair also saw a tiger on a trail early one morning near our camp before the battle. "It was really early, just before dawn," he said, "and a tiger walked out on the trail between the guy on point and the guy in front of me. We all stopped, and it just stood on the trail and looked at us. Then it walked on into the elephant grass."

At that time Vietnam probably had several thousand tigers, the Indochinese or "Corbett" kind, which aren't the largest tigers in the world. A big male usually weighs around four hundred pounds and will be about nine feet long (tail included), and the females might weigh near three hundred pounds and be about eight and a half feet long. But they were still the top predator in the Vietnamese food chain, and they lived in a lot of different kinds of places: forests, grasslands, mountains, and hills.

Tigers are said to be cunning, solitary, fierce, determined, and strong. They are really good at slipping quietly through the jungle and at ambushing their prey. That's how they hunt, prowling around mostly at night hiding in trees, tall grass, or some other cover till they spot something to eat, then they creep as close as possible to their prey, being careful to stay far enough away to avoid being discovered. That's when they jump—it's said they can leap more than thirty feet in a single pounce—taking the prey by surprise, so it has little chance to escape.

They try to grab their prey on the back, usually aiming for the neck area, and use their strong jaws and long, sharp teeth to either break a prey animal's neck or back or cut a major artery. If the prey doesn't die outright, the tiger hangs on to it until it bleeds to death or strangles it till it dies. They can also break a prey's back or skull with their big paws.

Tigers are also good at camouflage. Vietnamese tigers are dark orange or gold colored with narrow, dark stripes that help them blend into the plants and shadows.

I guess you could say we Green Berets were a lot like tigers—we were good at stealth and ambushes, we were determined and strong, and we had just proven in the camp that we were fierce. We also were good at camouflage. We even wore "tiger suits," our tiger-stripe uniforms.

This kind of striped camouflage uniform had been used by the French when they were fighting in Vietnam before us, and the South Vietnamese armed forces had continued to use a type of it for jungle fighting. These uniforms came in different patterns, but generally they were olive or khaki with sixty-four narrow green, brown, and black stripes. They really did help us blend into the jungle, so we Special Forces guys had adopted this type of uniform. In fact Carter, the Nungs, and I were all wearing these tiger suits when the battle began, and we still had what was left of them on that night, only they were tattered and torn and covered in blood, sweat, and all kinds of other grunge.

Now, normally tigers like to eat things like wild deer and pigs and sometimes smaller animals, like monkeys, porcupines, and badgers. But thanks to the war, they had added something new to their diets: the bodies of the dead soldiers from both sides left unburied in the jungle. These were prime pickings for tigers and they had learned to take advantage of that food source, helping themselves to the remains. In some cases they were even brave enough to go after living soldiers.

I recall hearing that, a year or two after I was at A Shau, two American servicemen were attacked, and one was reportedly killed, by tigers.

In our case, this tiger was probably drawn to us by the smell of our festering wounds and dried blood and might well have thought we were a good meal, so we had reason to be afraid of it, but there was not much we could do except sit there and hope it didn't attack. If we tried to scare it away or shoot it, that would alert the NVA to our location.

Maybe that tiger was too smart to jump us or maybe it decided to be on our side, but for whatever reason, it didn't attack. What it did do, though, was scare away the NVA soldiers who had surrounded us. They must have heard it or seen it, too, and the only thing I can figure is the enemy was more afraid of this tiger than they were of us. They backed off and we were gone again.

Thanks to that tiger, we were able to elude capture until, at about nine thirty on the morning of March 12, the weather broke enough that a helicopter found us and came in to pick us up. I can't remember just how we let the chopper know where we were or how we signaled them of our exact location, but somehow they found us.

Even though the tiger had made the NVA back off, they were still following us, so we had to work fast to chop a pad for the helicopter, which was traveling light. It had just the pilot and co-pilot, and it did not have any gunners with it, I suppose to make sure they had room for all of us.

They dropped strings for us and we all scrambled aboard, flying away just as the NVA trackers began to open fire on us. With no gunner on board, I started manning a machine gun and left a calling card with a few of them on the way out. As we flew away, I didn't see any signs of a tiger anywhere, but I was sure thankful it was out there and had shown up at the right time.

CHAPTER SIXTEEN

ON THE HOME FRONT

WHILE I WAS IN THE MIDDLE of this battle and the escape, my wife, Mary Arington Adkins, was at home with our four young boys, and none of them knew what was going on, or so I thought.

It was not unusual for Mary to have no idea where I was or what I was doing. That was a fact she accepted not long after we met on a blind date in 1955.

But let me go back and start at the beginning.

Mary was born on a farm, about seventy-five acres in size, out on the outskirts of Opelika, Alabama, where they raised pigs and cows and grew a garden, all to feed their family, which, like mine, was big—actually bigger—and hers was what they now call "blended."

Her father was a carpenter who worked mostly on houses, but also helped build the barracks at Fort Benning. Her mother was a stay-at-home mom who had her hands full. When they got married, Mary's father was a forty-four-year-old widower with seven kids. He and Mary's mother, who was twenty years younger than her new husband, had six more children together, of which Mary was the next to the youngest.

Also like me, Mary had a good life in that large family. "We were just plain people out on a farm, but we didn't know we were plain people out on a farm," she has often said. "We just enjoyed life."

How I came to meet Mary is kind of interesting. She was twenty-three when we met and she was working in one of the local sewing factories—Opelika was a mill town at that time—and Mary was friends with another girl who worked there. That girl was dating one of my buddies over at Fort Benning, where I was stationed at the time.

This buddy and I went over to Opelika one night in October to see his girlfriend (Mary's friend) and when we got there, we had her call Mary and say, "I've got somebody here who says he'd like to meet a nice girl. Would you like to come over?"

Mary did come over and evidently she liked me pretty well. We saw each other just about every night after that except when I went home to Oklahoma for the Christmas holidays. I tried to get Mary to go with me, but she said no since we had just started dating. She might as well have come with me, though, because we got married in her parents' living room on April 7, 1956, just about five months after we'd met.

Mary had a little house there in Opelika, close to her parents' house. Her father had given each of his kids three acres of land, and Mary had the house built and had just moved in when we got married. In fact, a little bit of it wasn't completed and we didn't have city water, so I got out there and dug a well by hand for us.

We lived there for more than four years, and during that time our first son was born, but when I volunteered for Special Forces we all loaded up and moved to Fort Bragg, North Carolina.

Now, Mary knew exactly what she was getting into with me being in the military. "I didn't go into it blind," she said. So she didn't mind moving to Fort Bragg, where our second son was born and where she settled in to military life, while I completed my Special Forces training and began to do some missions that took me away from home. By the time I left for my first tour in Vietnam, she was accustomed to being alone and handling things by herself. In fact, she was pregnant with our third child at that time, who was born two weeks after I left. She tells a funny story about that.

"My mother came over from Alabama to help with the older boys, so when I went to the hospital to deliver the baby, I had to go by myself. When I got in a room, the nurse came in and said, 'Is your husband here?' I said, 'No, he is Vietnam.' A little bit later the nurse came in checking me and said, 'Are you sure your husband isn't here?' I said, 'No, he's in Vietnam.' A third time she came in and said, 'There's a man out there in the hall. Are you sure that's not your husband?' I never found out who he was."

At that time the lines of communication between the United States and Vietnam were not great, and it was at least a month after the baby was born before I even knew whether it was a boy or a girl. It was another boy.

And that's the thing. Mary knew I was in Vietnam, but that's all she knew. As she says, "Once he left the house, when he left out the door, I had no idea where he was. I just knew he was gone. I think the only time I ever knew his whereabouts was when he left for a month to go to the mountains for training. And when he was in Vietnam, he was able to send me a letter once in a while, but that was about it."

But Mary accepted it. As she said, "I guess I just knew what I had gotten myself into when I married him and that's how it was going to be, plus I had kids to take care of and I couldn't sit down and feel sorry for myself. It was just something I had to do."

By the time I left for my second tour in Vietnam, the A Shau tour, we had four little boys and Mary really had her hands full, so she decided to go back to her house in Opelika while I was overseas, so she could be closer to her family.

So when I was in the Battle of A Shau, Mary was going about her daily business, getting the older boys off to school while the younger ones were still at home. She had no idea I had been in a battle until she got a telegram sometime around March 11 saying I was missing in action. At that time the military automatically sent MIA telegrams if a soldier had been out of contact for more than twenty-four hours.

The story goes that a neighbor saw a taxicab pull up in another neighbor's yard near our house in Opelika and realized it would not be carrying good news. Figuring it might be headed to our house, too, the neighbor immediately called Mary's oldest sister, Dot, who lived nearby, and got Dot's youngest daughter, Glenda, on the phone.

Dot and her middle daughter, Marcia, were shopping at the local Big Apple grocery store at the time, so Glenda called the store and told the manager to tell her mom to come home, then Glenda took off across the road to make sure someone was with Mary before the cab arrived.

Glenda remembers being there when the cab drove up to our house and can still describe the cab driver to this day. She said he was a chubby man with a big round belly, and he was wearing a western-type belt and boots and his hair was a comb-over. She said she would never forget him.

Marcia recalled that when the store manager found them in the store, he told Dot to just leave her grocery cart and go. Marcia also recalled that her mother put on her sunglasses to leave, and tears were just rolling down her face.

Sometime in the next day or so, though, Mary got what she took as good news. She got up that morning and was getting the boys ready for the day, when she turned on the television. That's when she heard the newscaster talking about these soldiers and a tiger. "Something hit me and I knew it had to be Ben," Mary said.

The newscaster didn't say anything about what happened to the men involved. All he said was that a tiger had gotten in between some American soldiers and the enemy. Right after Mary heard that news report, one of her nephews who lived close by came running over to the house. He had heard the news report, too, and was saying, "That's Uncle Ben. I know that's Uncle Ben."

A day or so later, Mary got another telegram saying I'd been found, but they had no idea what condition I was in. And a day after that she finally got a telegram saying I was in the hospital, but I was going to be okay. It was not until after I got home from A Shau that she knew the details of the battle.

When my family back in Oklahoma first got the news I was missing in action, most of them gathered at my parents' house to be together. But apparently my dad wasn't there. According to other family members' reports, my youngest brother, Jim, found him at a local bar. Now, my dad didn't drink in front of people and he didn't smoke, but my brother said he found him sitting at the bar, where he had been smoking and drinking for a while. He was in bad shape, and all he said was "Those damn Japs have killed my son."

I didn't know what the families of the other A Shau men were going through at that time, though years later some of the surviving men and their wives shared their stories with me.

Wayne Murray was not married at the time of A Shau, but he knew his parents had gotten word he was missing in action. He wanted them to know he was okay, so he walked over to where Walter Cronkite was interviewing people who had been in the battle and got himself on the news. "That's how they found out I was alive," he said.

Like Mary, Victor Underwood's wife, Diane, got the news of his situation by telegram. She and their two daughters were living in California with her parents, just about ten miles away from Vic's parents, while he was in Vietnam, which she said gave her a sense of security, especially after spending most of their lives up until then traveling as a military family.

When Underwood was sent to Vietnam, they both knew it was dangerous, but Diane also knew her husband was well trained and that he wanted to be part of the war effort, so she was determined not to worry. Still, Diane and her parents made it a point to not turn on the news.

"There was no way we were going to hear all the war news, because we couldn't do a thing about it," Diane said. "I would have really been a wreck if I had known all the terrible things that were happening there."

Diane kept herself and their daughters distracted by going to the zoo, the Monterey tide pools, and that sort of thing. She remembered her dad helped distract the girls, too. Some nights he would take the girls out in the pasture near their house and they would lie on the ground and look at the stars.

"Those were happy times," recalled Diane.

That changed on March 11, 1966, though. Diane's parents were out of the house, but she was home with their youngest daughter, who had come home on the bus around lunchtime after finishing her half day at kindergarten.

"There was a big picture window out the front of the house and in comes a taxi in our driveway," Diane said. "It was probably about one P.M. The taxi driver came up and said, 'I have a telegram for you,' then he turned around and got back in his car and left. I opened it."

Diane still has that telegram. It read:

March 11, 1966, 12:40 P.M.
Mrs. Diane Underwood,

The Secretary of the Army has asked me to express his deep regret that your husband, SFC Victor C.

Underwood has been missing in Vietnam since 10 March 1966. He was last seen engaged in [a] firefight with a hostile force.

You will be advised promptly when further information is received. A representative of the commanding general sixth US Army will contact you personally to offer assistance.

In order to protect any information which might be used to your husband's detriment, your cooperation is requested in making public only information concerning his name, rank, service number and date of birth.

J.C. Lambert Major General USA, The Adjutant General

For Diane, the fact that this telegram said Vic was missing in action—not killed—made it easier to read, but she immediately called her father at the car dealership he owned. He was not there, so she called her brother, who owned a nearby ice cream parlor, and he came to be with her.

"He came dashing up to the house and probably he drove at a hundred miles per hour to get there, knowing him," Diane said. Her mother came in shortly after that with groceries.

"I honestly can't remember anything after that," Diane said, even when her older daughter came home on the school bus. But she does remember having to tell her in-laws.

"I asked my brother if he would take me to Vic's parents' house, and as we drove down the hill and I saw people doing their normal activities I thought, 'What are those people doing? Why hasn't everything stopped?' I think it was my world that stopped."

When they arrived at the Underwood's house, Diane said, "There really wasn't much to say, and his father was taking it hard and was back in the bedroom, so I didn't stay long. They thought he was dead and they were taking the negative view, but I was taking the positive view."

"Here is how I felt: Vic was highly trained and I knew if he had a chance, he would be alive. I knew it. I never thought he was dead, never. If he could escape into the jungle, I was sure he knew how to take care of himself and survive."

She was right. "The next morning we were up early when the phone rang, and it was Vic's voice on the phone," she said. "A Red Cross lady got the phone call through to me."

According to Vic, Diane was so emotional he had to talk to her father. "I told him everything I could," he said, though Vic did minimize the extent of his injuries, which were pretty severe.

Within a few hours of that call, Diane got another telegram. It read:

March 12, 1966 10:32 A.M.
Mrs. Diane Underwood,

I am pleased to inform you that your husband Sergeant
First Class Victor C. Underwood avoided capture
during the encounter with hostile forces previously

reported to you and has returned to military control.
During the encounter he sustained a metal fragment
wound of the right leg. He is not repeat not seriously
wounded he was treated at 8th field hospital APO
San Francisco 96240 and is being held for further
treatment. Since he is not repeat not seriously wounded
no further reports will be furnished. Address mail to
him at the above medical facility.

J.C. Lambert Major General USA, The Adjutant
General

Again, I'm not sure how the other wives and families of A
Shau's men handled the aftermath of the battle but for almost
all of us, we did not make it home for several months to check
on them in person.

When I did get home, though, Mary spent weeks picking
little bits of shrapnel out of my arms and legs. "They were
down in his skin and every once in a while one would work
its way out and pop up," recalled Mary. "I'd take tweezers and
pull them out."

And she also showed me something she had received while I
was in Vietnam: a letter from the First Lady of South Vietnam.

The letter was written in English and addressed to Mary.
"It was just the kind of letter that one woman would write to
another woman saying how she felt and that she knew how I
felt about Ben being away."

"I think she was just reaching out and why she picked me
I will never, never, never know," Mary said. "And how she

knew me and where to send the letter to me was a mystery. I just know it was really a nice letter. A very nice letter."

I carried the letter to the base and turned it in to my commanding officer. We never saw it again. I guess they sent it to Washington and Washington kept it.

It was during that time we got some other news, too. We found out I had been recommended for the Medal of Honor for my efforts at A Shau, but that was not a priority for any of us. We had work to do and a family to raise. I did receive the Distinguished Service Cross for that battle, which I wore proudly because there were not many of those awarded.

CHAPTER SEVENTEEN

NO REST FOR THE WEARY

A LOT HAD HAPPENED TO ALL OF US at Camp A Shau, but when the battle was over there was still a lot going on for those of us who survived, and for many of us the first order of business was to attend to our wounds.

Each of us was taken to a different place once we were evacuated, and I'm not sure about all of the men who survived the battle, but here's what I know about some of them.

Dave Blair was flown back to Hue where he, Mari, and Hoover were eating lunch by about eleven thirty on March 12. Blair was not too severely injured, but he got out of the camp with very little but the clothes on his back. "Other than my harness, the only thing I had that was mine was my watch, which had gotten broken during the course of the battle, and my underwear."

Vic Underwood was taken to a hospital in Nha Trang, where the medic who triaged him was not optimistic about the condition of Vic's right leg. It was badly wounded, covered in leech holes, yellow from the knee down, and he couldn't feel his foot. There was some talk of amputation as they took Underwood into surgery, but when he came out of that he still had both legs.

"The doctor told me those leeches probably saved the leg," said Underwood. "They had sucked the poison out."

From the battle Pointon and Wayne Murray were immediately taken to a medical facility, probably in Phu Bai, where Murray spent one night before he was transferred to Da Nang for further treatment. But during the night he was robbed.

"I got out of the camp with a buck knife, my combat equipment, a flack vest, a Thai silver cigarette lighter, my identification card, and twenty dollars in military payment certificates [MPCs]," he said. "After that first night all I had left was my ID card. They stole my knife, they stole my MPCs, they stole my lighter. I had no clothes. An ID card was all that I had left in the world."

Murray spent about a week and a half at a naval hospital in Da Nang where he was treated for his wounds, including broken metacarpal bones in his hand.

George Pointon, whose injuries were probably the most severe of all us survivors, was taken to Da Nang where his clothes were cut off his body so they could get to his wounds.

"I must have passed out for a couple of hours, but when I woke up I'm lying there in my underwear and I thought, 'Where's that letter?'"

The letter Bao had given Pointon at the stream was gone. Pointon would never have a chance to give it to Bao's family.

From there Pointon was transferred to the Philippines, where they were planning to send him on to Walter Reed Medical Center back in the States. He had a girlfriend in Okinawa, though, so somehow Pointon talked them into sending him there instead. But when he got there, Pointon found he was not very interested in having company.

"People would come visit me," he said, "but I didn't want to see anyone. I was so miserable and I hurt so much. I couldn't concentrate on anything other than the pain. It was an evil pain."

He recalled lying in the hospital and hearing the music of bands playing at local clubs and people would ask him, "Don't you want to be there at the club?"

"I thought, 'No, I want to be right here,'" Pointon said. "I didn't want to be anyplace but in an intensive care unit, because that was the only place I could come to grips with the pain."

Pointon's recovery was long—in fact, it took two years or more and went six or seven surgeries to get him back into commission, and he still suffers from pain; during the first several weeks in Okinawa, he lost sixty pounds.

He remembered seeing himself for the first time after those initial weeks of recovery. "Understand that for the first five or six weeks, all I could do was use a little mirror to shave," he said. When he was finally able to get up and walk a little bit, he remembers going down a hallway for physical therapy.

"I looked up and I saw this guy coming at me and I am thinking, 'Man, am I lucky. I'm in bad shape but look at this asshole. He looks like he just came off a death march or something.'

"I kept walking and then I realized that there was a full-length mirror at the end of the hall and I was looking at myself," Pointon said. "I passed out. When you go from being one hundred and sixty-five pounds to one hundred and five pounds and you haven't seen yourself in two months, it's scary."

Bradford was also taken to a hospital in Okinawa where he received treatment for his wounds, including the one on his buttocks. Though he had to stay there a pretty good while before he was considered "well," Bradford apparently felt well enough to leave his bed.

"I was sitting on the roof of the hospital drinking illicit booze that had been smuggled in to me by my cousin, and I am looking over at a sign flashing 'Texas Bar,' 'Texas Bar,' 'Texas Bar,' and there was another one over there flashing 'Tattoo,' 'Tattoo,'" he said. The temptation was too great.

"I climbed down a fire escape, I don't know how many floors, in my pajamas and a hospital diaper and I went to get a tattoo," he continued. "They had debrided the wounds in my ass and every day they'd pour Betadine in there and stuff it with gauze, then I would take a sitz bath and they would redo it again."

When he got to the tattoo parlor, Bradford asked for a Ranger tab tattoo on his backside and dropped his pajama bottoms. The tattoo artist saw Bradford's Betadine-stained backside and tried to say no, but Bradford insisted. After the tattoo was done, Bradford somehow snuck back into the hospital without being caught, but the next day when the nursing assistant was giving Bradford his sitz bath and saw the tattoo, she let out a howl and went and got a doctor.

"The doctor asked, 'Where did you get that?' I said, 'Where do you think?'" Bradford said. "They wanted to court-martial me, but the chaplain from the 1st got me off the hook."

After we were pulled out of the jungle, Carter and I were taken straight to a camp near Hue where they gave us a quick medical check and some food, but at that point we couldn't eat much. If you do without food for that long a time you have no space or desire for it, though once you do start eating again it seems like you can't stop.

I can't recall what I had with me when I left the camp, but I know that when they pulled me on the helicopter my clothes were torn all over and I was super smelly, dirty, and bloody. I didn't even have an ID because I had left my wallet, which had my ID in it, lying by my bunk when the battle started, and I never bothered to go back for it. I have no idea what happened to my ol' sawed-off shotgun, either, but I never saw it again after I got to Phu Bai.

I also don't know what happened to Carter after we got to Hue because they sent me to a medical ship, the USS *Repose*, the hospital ship that went from Da Nang to the Philippines. They sent me there because a shrapnel wound to my left eye had become infected, and they did not have qualified eye doctors on the mainland.

I think it was on the ship that they counted up all the wounds I had from the battle. They said there were eighteen, but most of them were caused by shrapnel from the artillery and hand grenades and none of them were super severe.

I was on the ship for two or three days, and during that time the ship made the trip to the Philippines where I was given a clean uniform, and then I was sent back to Vietnam.

It wasn't long after, all of us apparently having recovered well enough from our injuries, that Sam Carter, Victor Underwood, and I were assigned the mission to make the restitution payments for the Nungs who had been killed in the battle. That was a horrible, horrible assignment that eventually took about two weeks, but before we really got started doing that, we were debriefed about what had happened during the battle, especially what had happened with the indigenous troops.

I had so many debriefings with flag officers and other officers down the chain of command that I lost count, and the media was there, too. I was never allowed to talk to the media, probably because my comments would have been derogatory toward the South Vietnamese, but others did.

Dave Blair talked to them almost immediately after he was rescued from the jungle. "When I got off the chopper in Hue, I think every reporter in Vietnam must have been there and, of course, I was pretty tired and angry," he said. "The reporters asked me some questions and I wish somebody had told me to shut up, but I complained about the cowardly leader [Dung] and the 141 Company that had defected on us. My emotions were running rather high."

Wayne Murray also got almost immediate media attention. A picture of Murray being carried off his rescue helicopter ran in *Newsweek* magazine on March 28, 1966, and there's another United Press International photo of him with a cast on his hand talking to the media just a few days after the battle, which he had agreed to do so his parents would know that he was still alive.

"They got me out of the hospital, put a Specialist 6 uniform on me, and had me talk to Walter Cronkite," Wayne recalled. Cronkite and other news media were on the ground there covering the story of the battle and already knew there had been problems with the South Vietnamese soldiers in the camp during the battle. Someone in the media even called it the "Alamo of Vietnam."

"I'm sitting there with a cast on my hand and I have a sergeant major of the C detachment, the commander of the 5th Special Forces, and the C Team commander standing behind me while they are asking questions about the South Vietnamese. I knew Cronkite wanted me to say they were all craven cowards and they ran, but I wouldn't say it. Some were good, some were bad."

Around that time several of us were also brought in to testify as part of an official Article 32 hearing investigating what happened during the battle. The investigation, which is like a preliminary hearing in a civilian court, was focused on the possible court-martial of the Marine helicopter commander Chuck House, for his order to shoot "friendlies" during the evacuation chaos.

"When they brought us in for this, I had a pair of borrowed fatigues on and I didn't even have a belt," recalled Underwood. "I wasn't prepared to go and report to any general. But one of the Marines gave me a belt and then they called me in there."

"I reported to the president of the board, a Marine one-star general who had been awarded the Medal of Honor from

WWII—a fighter pilot," Underwood recalled. "I think he was the deputy division commander of the Marine division. And there was an army general sitting in there with tape recorders. I took one look at him and I knew he was somebody from the Pentagon. He looked like he just stepped out of a duffle bag."

Underwood recalls that, after he reported what he knew about the shootings to the board, one of the generals (he thinks it was the Medal of Honor recipient) on that board got up and came around the table. "He shook my hand and said, 'I wish I had more NCOs like you,'" Underwood said. "That's the best compliment I think I have ever had in my life."

All any of us could say to the board was that the South Vietnamese who were shot had fought with the enemy, so they were the enemy and were treated the same way as the enemy. That seemed to satisfy the board at the hearing. I never heard anything else about that investigation.

After that we all went about paying the death gratuities, which was probably harder on Underwood than it was for me, since Vic had worked super closely with the Nungs on the Mike Force. He had a great respect for them and had even written an account of their actions on Red Cross stationery while he was laid up in the hospital.

In that account, Underwood praised the efforts of the Nungs throughout the battle, pointing out that they helped aid and protect wounded Americans and also fought bravely throughout the battle. Vic wrote that, after some of the indigenous troops had abandoned their 4.2 mortar position leaving all the ammo with it, "one Nung soldier, without orders, crawled under heavy fire to the pit and set fire to the ammo, destroying the gun, ammo, and himself."

He also pointed out how the Nungs had helped during the chaotic evacuation. "I observed the Nungs helping the wounded, including Americans, aboard the helicopters knowing full well that there would not be room for themselves," Underwood wrote in this account. "The Nungs very definitely and without a doubt proved that they are among the best fighters in Vietnam today and I feel very proud to have had the opportunity to work, fight, bleed, and cry over the dead and missing as one of them."

It was that kind of thing that made those restitution payments so hard to deliver. And it was something that the Mike Force had to do frequently during the Vietnam War. Though John Bradford was still in the hospital, so he wasn't able to help us make those payments, he later recalled another occasion when he was sent down to the Cho Lon district of Saigon, an area where the Chinese were concentrated, to pay some.

"They had a gal there called the 'Dragon Lady' who recruited personnel for us. When you paid a death gratuity, you went to her and she probably took a piece of it, but she would hire professional mourners," Bradford said. "One time we saw them put a Nung's body up on a flatbed truck and they drove it around with the incense burning and these people were yelling and screaming. It was quite a ceremonial thing."

To me, paying the restitutions was especially hard because the majority of the time the families didn't know their loved one had died, and they sure didn't want to see us. I imagine seeing us show up in their neighborhood was like seeing a taxi cab pull up at our families' doors. It couldn't be good news.

I don't really know what happened to the CIDG and LLDB men who survived A Shau, though I understand that Dung, the South Vietnamese Special Forces commander who didn't fight real well during the battle, and who was one of the first men on a helicopter when we were being evacuated, was sent to a camp close to the Special Forces headquarters.

At some point, Dave Blair heard he was there and wanted to get even.

"Mari and I were in the barracks and when I was told Dung was in camp," said Blair, "I put a round in my pistol and undid the flap on it. Then I went up to him and called him a coward and every vile thing I could think of. I tried to provoke him into drawing on me so I could have a Wild West shootout with him."

According to Blair, Dung did not take the bait and was able to walk away from that one, but later he was seen at another camp by some of the Nungs who had been in the battle where so many of them had fought and died or been wounded. All I know is that Dung became a casualty of war shortly thereafter. I have no direct knowledge of what happened, though.

When we got through paying the restitutions, which took about ten days to two weeks, I was reassembled with Dave Blair, Lew Mari, Vernon Carnahan, and Herril Robbins, and we were sent into the Tien Phuoc area, which was near Da Nang, to do the same thing all over again.

We were all doing okay by then, except Robbins who was just not all there. He would go around looking at the mountains, and he probably should have been sent out of the country for medical help, but it was just not available at the time. I understand that eventually he committed suicide once he got back home.

At Tien Phuoc we also received some replacements to our team to fill in for those who had been severely wounded or killed at A Shau. One of those was a Special Forces medic, a big six-foot-one guy who spent a month or so with us, and then was assigned to another team. He was shot and captured when he was with that team and spent five years as a prisoner of war. I saw him again for the first time a few years ago in Portland, Oregon, and he told me that when they released him he weighed eighty-seven pounds. That was a reminder about why we Special Forces men are determined to never be taken prisoner.

I was doing intelligence work again while we were in Tien Phuoc, and we were definitely in the thick of bad things and in another place where it was really hard to tell the good guys from the bad ones.

For example, there was a Buddhist priest who came into camp a lot, and he always seemed to show up and start talking to someone when a briefing was going on. It became so obvious that I was pretty sure he was an NVA agent, but they would not let us take him as a prisoner, which would have been the best so we could get information out of him, or eliminate him. I understand some other organization got him, though.

Another example is that four or five hundred yards across the river from our camp was a row of houses we started getting fire from. It turned out to be six or eight women soldiers, the first time we had run into a unit of all women. That was kind of difficult for us to handle, and our gunships would not return fire because they were women, but the house was eventually destroyed and we captured one of the women. She was tough and difficult to interrogate, but she probably thought she was going to be killed anyway.

Another time there was this woman and her daughter who sold snacks at the camp. We found out later they were also mining the roads in the area.

There was also a monument of Ho Chi Minh in that area and we found a cave near it. The civilians in town would run into the cave, which we wanted to destroy, but our commanding officers wouldn't let us do it. I came to find out later it was one of the tunnels the NVA was using as an infiltration route.

There were also some unusual threats and ways to get hurt there. I was on one patrol and we were going up a mountain when the Vietnamese soldiers with me spotted something. I thought it was just a mine, but someone took a stick and punched it. It was a big bear trap. We carried it out, and I think it became a souvenir for one of our soldiers.

We did sometimes have some fun at those Special Forces camps, though. A group of Australian musicians actually came out to A Shau before the battle, and I remember seeing the actress and singer Martha Raye perform at one of our camps. Bob Hope would come into higher headquarters and places that were secure, but Martha Raye would come out to the camps. She was not afraid of anything.

Raye was a strong supporter of Special Forces. In fact, she had a room in her house in California where any Special Forces soldier was welcome to stay. She was later made an honorary colonel in the Special Forces and there is a room dedicated to her at the Special Forces museum at Fort Bragg.

Sometime at the end of July or first of August 1966 they sent me home, and at that point they changed jobs on me. I was no longer an intelligence sergeant. They made me a team sergeant, and they decided at that time I would become a special operations man.

CHAPTER EIGHTEEN

TWO MONTHS AND TWENTY MINUTES

WHILE I WAS PAYING restitutions and then moved on to Tien Phuoc, Wayne Murray had another assignment that was even harder. He, Victor Underwood, and Sam Carter returned to Camp A Shau to retrieve the remains of our fallen men.

The recovery mission, named "Operation Blue Star," occurred on May 14, 1966, about two months after the battle. According to the Operation Blue Star operational report, which remained classified until 1996, the stated mission of the operation was "to recover five USASF bodies" and "bury indigenous bodies lying in the open, without further loss of US lives."

Before they sent anyone back in, air reconnaissance had been done in the area and the recon indicated the NVA had been in and out of the ruined camp several times since the battle ended, but their activity seemed to have died down. However, it was a pretty good bet the NVA or Viet Cong in the area were keeping it under surveillance.

The report also stated it was likely the bodies and equipment that remained there had been booby-trapped and trip lines for mines had been laid. There was also a good chance snipers might be in the area, but it did not appear that a large NVA force was close by the camp and, if smaller forces were around it, they probably would not attempt an ambush.

If they did try to ambush the Blue Star team, it was estimated such an attack could be "neutralized" by air support for at least thirty minutes while our men were on the ground. But that meant the composite force of Special Forces personnel sent into the camp, with support from air force and Marine helicopters, had only thirty minutes to complete the mission.

The team was divided into three details: one for security, one for recovery of the US bodies, and a third for burial of all indigenous soldiers' bodies. They had a specific protocol about how to handle things, too, including the following:

No object will be moved without first being disturbed by a grappling hook; all such disturbances will be preceded by the call "FIRE IN THE HOLE," a five-second delay, then "CLEAR."

All US bodies will be tagged, located on photos, and identifying items collected prior to movement. Only medical personnel will move US bodies.

A close count will be kept on all indigenous bodies buried.

Wayne Murray went in as part of the security detail, Sam Carter and Victor Underwood were part of the burial detail, and Lewis Mari was part of the team sent in to specifically recover Taylor's body.

Dave Blair and I wanted to go in with them but they wouldn't let us, plus Blair was super sick from dysentery, which he had gotten from drinking out of that mud puddle outside the camp, and Dengue fever.

The whole operation was "a rather tricky thing," Wayne Murray told me later. "A Caribou came in and landed in Tien Phuoc and I got on it. We flew up to Da Nang the next morning and then on up to Phu Bai, where we got on helicopters and went out. My group was put in on the north side. I remember that it smelled like nuoc mam and burning shit."

"We swept the area," Murray continued. "I worked my way to the west side of the camp and once we decided it was secure, I popped a green smoke [the signal that the position was suitable as a landing zone] and the helicopters came in with the body bags."

According to Vic Underwood, there was more to the operation than body recovery and burial. "Supposedly we went in to bury the bodies, but that was a bunch of bullshit," he said. "My mission when we went in was to check out the North Vietnamese. We did have grappling hooks with fifty feet of line on them and we could hook it on a body and move it, but the bodies were all decayed."

According to Murray, the NVA had already policed up all of the bodies of their troops, so all that was left were the bodies of the Americans and some of the South Vietnamese. But these had been picked over, and some of the CIDG bodies had been piled up. The NVA had also disassembled our generators and hauled off their parts and parts off our trucks, including the tires they probably used to make shoes (those tire sandals we called "Ho Chi Minh slippers").

When Wayne got to the team house, which had been burned to the ground, he poked around in the rubble. "Mari had left his class ring in the safe and I was looking for the safe, but I couldn't find it. It was gone. I did find an old Schmeisser submachine gun that had been hanging up on the wall and I brought it back. It was a little bit rusty, but it was still there."

Murray also said the big concrete bunker on the west side of the camp was split from mortar fire and had filled with water. There may have been some Vietnamese bodies in it, too, but Wayne did not look. "After two months out there, the bodies would not have been in good shape," he said.

The team was able to bring home the bodies of some of the indigenous soldiers, though those bodies were hard to identify because they did not wear dog tags or other forms of identification. When we dealt with bodies, we respected their culture and religions and tried in every way we could to return the bodies to their homes. Sometimes this was accomplished and sometimes it was not.

According to Murray, the entire mission took twenty minutes, and they got all of the American bodies in the camp except for Jimmy Taylor, which still bothers me to this day.

Like I said, they didn't let me go in for the recovery and I don't know why, but the bottom line is I knew where Taylor's body was and I might have been able to find it. Carter knew, too, but I'm not sure he would have remembered because that night he was in such horrible shape physically.

"Mari knew exactly where Taylor's body was because we had taken coordinates," said Vic Underwood later, "but the body was gone. He could have been consumed by animals. Those animals were getting fat around all that combat."

According to Murray, being back at the camp had not bothered him while they were there for the recovery mission. But that night it did.

"We flew back to Da Nang where I was spending the night before we flew out the next day to Tien Phuoc and I was taking my boots off. I smelled my hand and I smelled the death on it," said Wayne. "I tossed my cookies."

Though Murray had done many brave things during the battle, he said going back in after the fact was his most heroic act.

"That was the bravest thing I did because I didn't have to do that. I volunteered to do it because I felt I owed it to the families of the people who were killed there," Murray said.

CHAPTER NINETEEN

TRAINING FOR STEALTH; RETURNING TO ACTION

WHEN I GOT BACK from my second tour in July or August of 1967, I still had a number of painful wounds from the battle. I had healed pretty quickly, which I think is because I was fit and toned to the point there was nothing to prevent the healing.

I also had the best medical care in the world, and I was also fortunate that my sergeant major at Fort Bragg who was a three-war man—World War II, Korea, and Vietnam—took good care of me. They wanted to send me downrange again too quickly and he wouldn't let them. He took me under his wing and guided me for my first five or six months back at Bragg. He made sure I got well.

When he finally said I was ready to go again, I was one of about twenty or thirty Special Forces people pulled aside for some special training. They wouldn't tell us what was going on with this, but two or three us who had been downrange before had a pretty good idea based on the type of training we were getting.

While I was in Vietnam for that second tour, I had gone on one super top-secret mission to A Luoi. They told everyone I was wounded to get me out of A Shau for that mission, which I cannot talk about, but it was a top-secret mission and it gave me an idea of what happened when you were part of the Studies and Observation Group (SOG).

Our training at Fort Bragg seemed to indicate that's where I might be going next because they had us working with weapons that had sound suppressors, what some people call "silencers," on them, which was something we didn't usually use in combat.

A good example is one we called a "grease gun" or a "Swedish K," though its official name is a 9 mm Carl Gustav M/45 submachine gun, which has a big screw-on barrel that is the sound suppressor. I never did like those guns because the ones we were using at that time did not have safeties on them. Anything could catch the trigger and it would fire. But it was a real fast-firing weapon and the ammunition it used was lighter weight, so you could carry more.

We were also doing a tremendous amount of physical training, and they were teaching us more tactics for the jungle for absolute stealth. I learned how to move so slow through the jungle that it seemed like I might not move but fifteen feet in a day. I also learned how to be super quiet. Before I ever put a foot down, I learned to look and see where that foot was going.

In other words, I learned how to make sure I didn't make any noise that would give me away to the enemy.

During our training, we had a chance to learn a number of specialized techniques as well. For example, as part of our SERE training we were taught how to use a new modified version of the McGuire Rig, an aerial extraction system that uses looped ropes to lift up to three men at a time out of a hot spot. At one point, they also sent us out into the Piedmont area of North Carolina to do field training again, but the only problem with that was it was wintertime in North Carolina, so there was snow and ice and they were trying to prepare us for jungle missions. That didn't work too well.

I remember the funny thing was there was so much snow and ice that they cancelled the operation, but they couldn't get to us. They were worried we didn't have enough food, but somewhere in the mountains we found somebody's empty cabin and we killed a couple of deer. We were living good, but that was not the best "jungle" training.

Based on all this kind of training, I figured out we were going to be working for the Military Assistance Command, Vietnam—Studies and Observations Group (MACV-SOG), which conducted missions so top-secret you weren't there.

SOG was first created in January 1964 to conduct strategic reconnaissance missions in North and South Vietnam, Laos, and Cambodia. They did things like conduct psychological operations, go on undercover missions, capture enemy prisoners, and rescue downed pilots and prisoners of war in all those countries, and in other countries, too. SOG was also part of most of the major campaigns during the Vietnam War, like

the Gulf of Tonkin incident that happened before the war officially started and the Tet and Easter offensives.

At one time, SOG teams were also used during those years
when plane hijacking became so common. They not only went
in as a reaction force to get hostages and aircraft back, but they
also would go undercover on flights to help stop a hijacking.
I heard they stopped letting SOG do this after someone tried
to hijack a plane with Special Forces guards on it, and somewhere at about thirty-five thousand feet over the Caribbean a
door came open on the plane.

MACV-SOG reported directly to the Pentagon's Joint
Chiefs of Staff, and their work was so secret its existence was
denied by the US government for many years. John L. Plaster,
who served three one-year tours with MACV-SOG in Vietnam, wrote a book about this called *SOG: The Secret Wars of
America's Commandos in Vietnam* that tells a lot of the stories
from that time.

His book includes the exploits of some famous SOG men,
including the legendary Jerry "Mad Dog" Shriver, who became the poster boy for crazy Green Berets (and was a friend
of George Pointon) and Medal of Honor recipients Fred Zabi-
tosky, Jon Cavaiani, Roy Benavidez, and Robert Howard.

The way SOG worked was they would put together small
reconnaissance teams of usually ten or fewer people who would
go in for a mission, but the teams usually did not really know
what their mission was all about.

During my time in Special Forces I did some of these secret missions a number of times, and not just in Vietnam.
One such mission, one that falls in the category of "I was not
there," was when the United States was preparing to go into

the Dominican Republic in 1965. On that mission, two of us Special Forces guys were put on a navy plane and we landed in a lake in the Dominican Republic, where we were to meet a small boat and hand a package to the people in the boat. That package, now that I think about it, was probably US currency. We had the contingency plan that, if the plane couldn't get away, we had to escape and evade by land out of the country, but fortunately the plane did take off.

Another mission occurred between my second and third deployments to Vietnam, probably around 1969, when I made a night jump into Africa and linked up with some guerilla forces there that we were to help train and equip to overthrow the government.

While I was on that mission, they sent me into a local village, a place where I didn't exactly blend in with the local residents' skin color, to try and get some supplies, but I ran into another Special Forces soldier that I had served with in the past. I got to talking with him and asked him what he was doing there.

He said, "Since we've served together I won't have to shoot you. We're here training the government troops to destroy the rebels."

Whether this was because different agencies were working at odds on this, or because our government knew about this and wanted the good will of whoever won, or didn't care who won so they were covering both sides to make sure we had support there, I don't know. I just did my job and didn't ask questions.

What I did know about SOG in Vietnam was this: the missions were dangerous. They were so dangerous, in fact, that there was a more than 100 percent casualty rate among SOG soldiers. Pretty much every man was wounded, usually multiple times, and more than half of them died while on a SOG mission. But they were also good at what they did and had the highest kill ratio in US military history. According to Plaster, it was nearly 160:1 in 1970.

The men who were in SOG were a breed unto themselves. They were not chosen by pay grade or rank, but by ability, and it took a certain kind of person to do that kind of work.

Now, SOG was supposed to be an all-volunteer group, and in this case the "all volunteer" meant someone else volunteered us. In my case I was "volunteered" by a Colonel Dave Cole. I had worked with Cole in the past at Fort Bragg on his A Team when he was a captain, and apparently he asked for me specifically, so I didn't have any choice. I did say, "I didn't volunteer for this," but they said, "That doesn't make any difference. The commander has asked for you."

So when I got to Vietnam for my third tour, I was assigned to Command and Control North (CCN), which had its headquarters in Da Nang where I was briefed on what I was going to be doing. After that I was sent to Phu Bai Combat Base (also known as Phu Bai Airfield), which was about eight miles from Hue. This was a big military base that had been home to a number of different units since it was established in 1962, but by the time I was there in 1971 it was headquarters for the 101st Airborne Division.

Though it was a busy place with lots of other military operations going on at and around the base, our SOG unit was using it as a launch site for our missions, and we were sort of hiding there in plain sight, which was not easy.

Even though we wore sterile uniforms—ones with no rank, medals, or insignia—we had a hard time keeping our identity hidden on base, especially when we were trying to get our people in and out for a mission without being noticed by all the other military and civilian people on the base. They were always wondering what we were doing, especially when we brought aircraft in.

A SOG A Team, the one that carried out the mission on the ground, typically consisted of three Americans, usually all Special Forces soldiers. One served as the team leader for a mission and was called the "one-zero," another was the assistant leader or the "one-one," and the third man was the "one-two." Most of the time just two of these three men would go out on a mission at a time, and they would be accompanied by several Vietnamese soldiers, usually the ethnic, mainstream Vietnamese rather than the indigenous men.

SOG teams got their mission orders from somewhere in higher headquarters, but those orders had to go all the way to the Pentagon for approval, and sometimes the US president had to sign off on the decision before they were handed to a team.

The assignments could be anything, including going after a specific target, but most of the time they were reconnaissance missions, the most dangerous kinds of missions because you never knew what you'd drop into.

To prepare for a mission, all team members, including those riding air support, went through a very rigorous briefing process, often in isolation, just before and after a mission. During a briefing we were supplied with only the information pertinent to our specific job. For me, being in isolation was frustrating because I always wanted more information than I could get, but the bottom line was we were just locked up until it was time to launch a mission. The same sort of thing would happen when we got back from a mission—if we got back from one. We were debriefed and that was absolutely in isolation, too.

After the pre-mission briefing, the teams had to come up with a plan, which then had to be okayed by the commander. If he didn't okay it, the team had to go back and revise the plan. The one-zero always determined the amount of ammo and ordinance he wanted to take, but each team member had their own preference of weapons and other gear.

Teams always went in on a mission sterile—no tabs, insignias, badges, or name tags on their uniforms. No dog tags. Nothing that might identify them as Americans. In fact, sometimes they went in wearing NVA uniforms and carrying NVA weapons. I might have done that a time or two myself, but this was super dangerous because American units would shoot at you.

The team members all carried cameras, which at the time for us were Leicas because they were lightweight, and they often carried little mini grenades I never saw anywhere else in the military. These were so small you could carry ten or twelve in your belt instead of two of the usual size. They were not as strong as a larger grenade, but they worked really well on personnel. Some folks also carried things like claymore mines.

I was a master sergeant by then and a senior NCO, so my primary job was to put the SOG teams in and get them out, though I also went on some missions at times.

We would usually "put in" teams by air, though at times SOG men were known to walk into an area, paddle into it on a stream or river at night, or even ride a motorcycle in, though that didn't work too well because they could hear you coming.

To do an air drop, we used what we called a "package" of aircraft, which included four helicopters (we called them "slicks"), two gunships, and a fixed-wing Covey airplane. The way this worked was we would send in one gunship making a low run while the other stayed up higher. As soon as the first gunship had made its run, the other one would come in low on the other side. This went on constantly as cover while we used three of the slicks to put the recon team on the ground.

The majority of the time the insertion site was so small we could only put one slick in at a time. It dropped down to almost ground level, and the team jumped out of the heli-copter and took their positions. The fourth slick had a chase medic in it flying upstairs, circling and available to come in if needed. The whole mission was then directed by someone in the Covey, usually called the Covey "rider," who ran the radio to contact the men on the ground and also to call in backup, such as fast-movers (fighter jets) or Puff the Magic Dragons.

After a team was on the ground as many aircraft as pos-sible stayed close by in case they were compromised, which happened frequently because a lot of times NVA or VC were hiding in spider holes at a put-in site, and they would jump up and try to shoot the helicopters and the team. Because this was so common, we always did false insertions. In other words, we might "insert" three times, but only one of them would actu-ally put men on the ground, so the idea was the NVA would never know which one was the real team.

If an A Team was compromised, then we had to abort the mission and try to go back in and get them, and we lost a lot of men that way, both the ones on the ground and those in the air. If they weren't compromised, though, the team members took off and started implementing the mission plan.

Though most of the aircraft in the package left at this point, the Covey stayed around and kept in radio contact with the teams on the ground, which was usually done through a secure, scrambled radio. A lot of times, though, the Covey rider was the only one doing any talking. The A Team would answer by "breaking squelch"—one squelch meant yes, two squelches meant no.

For instance, one of the teams put in on a mission found themselves sitting in an enemy compound. The team leader in the Covey asked, "Do you want to bring them out?"

The SOG soldier squelched twice for "No."

"Are you secure?"

Two more squelches: "No."

"What are you doing?"

Silence.

Finally the guy was able to come on and say, "I'm sitting on a stump and I will be here for about two days." The NVA were all around him.

We usually tried to put a team in for just three to five days at a time because that's how much food they could carry with them. Water was not usually a problem, especially in the I Corps area where there were a lot of streams, but many SOG men wouldn't go near the streams because that's where the NVA might be.

There were some outposts, however, where SOG men might be sent for longer time periods. For example, we had a number of isolated radio relay stations used to guide the SOG teams and intercept communications from the NVA. They all had code names like "Lightning" and "Hickory," and I know there were a couple in South Vietnam, and there might have been one or two across the border, too.

There's a funny story about one of those that happened to this young lieutenant who later became a police chief in Home-wood, Alabama. He told me he showed up for a mission with no idea of what he was going to be doing. Someone put him on an aircraft that delivered him to a radio relay station where they left him for a month before he finally got a message say-ing, "Lieutenant, you've been AWOL for thirty days. You're in the wrong place."

Putting men in was always hard, but getting them out again after a mission, or if they were compromised, was even harder. It had to be done at night and the way it worked was the team set off a green smoke to let us know their location. Of course, the NVA and Viet Cong figured this out, and they would do the same thing to try and lure in a helicopter so they could shoot it down. It took a brave helicopter pilot to do that work and many of the helicopter pilots didn't like to do it, though we had a couple of South Vietnamese pilots who would go any-where, anytime. They picked up many where others said you couldn't go. One of them came out one time with eighty-some-thing bullet holes in his helicopter.

These missions were so tough it became a tradition that, if you were doing recon, you didn't talk about it until you had three missions under your belt. If you survived five, you had an opportunity to be the one-zero. (If you became a one-zero it didn't matter what rank you were; it was based on your ability and experience in the jungle. The one-zero was the boss.) If you lived through fifteen missions, everyone wondered how you had survived.

A lot of them didn't survive, of course, but they just kept sending these men back and back and back and back, so the truth was they were all living on borrowed time.

CHAPTER TWENTY

ON A MISSION; A PRICE ON MY HEAD

DURING MY TIME IN SOG, we did a lot of highly classified missions that involved inserting teams outside of Vietnam into a neutral country, and many times we did not have permission from those countries to be there. But the North Vietnamese were there and we needed to know what they were doing.

Pretty much every mission at that time was dangerous and often did not go well. For example, one time we had a team that went in a little bit south and west of the old Special Forces A Shau camp where I was in 1966. The team was compromised real early in the mission and we tried an extraction for them, but the NVA or Viet Cong shot the helicopters down and it looked like the whole team was lost.

About a day later, though, one of our beepers came up—the SOG team members carried locator beacons called "beepers"—and I sent a team to recover the beeper.

Afterward, I got in a lot of trouble because our higher headquarters didn't like that at all. They figured more than likely the NVA had stolen the beeper and was using it to lure in our helicopters so they could shoot them down, which happened often. My thought, though, was that one of our men was still out there.

In this case, the beeper happened to belong to a SOG man named Sammy Hernandez, one of the first Special Forces soldiers to make a combat HALO jump. Hernandez was part of the A Team on that mission who, during the attempted extraction, was riding strings. As he was being lifted out of the area beneath the helicopter, the rope snapped and he fell back into the jungle, where he was unconscious for a period of time. When he came to, though, he still had his beeper and cut it on. We brought him out as the only survivor of that team. I don't think we ever got all of the bodies from that mission out.

Like I said, higher headquarters didn't like me sending a team in after him, but Sammy will argue that with you now. He retired as a command sergeant major and lives in Georgia. He is a fine man and was a fine soldier.

But Hernandez's experience was mild compared to some of the other things that happened to SOG men. It got to the point that if the NVA ever wounded an American, they would cut him open while he was alive and sometimes burn him with a flamethrower, attempting to get someone else to come after him. This was the type of thing the recon people had to face.

That happened to a fine master sergeant I knew who was on a recon when his team was hit heavy and he had to "lay chilly" (stay perfectly still) in a hole somewhere. The NVA captured his other team members, and they were trying to get him out by treating the other two soldiers super bad. The master sergeant followed orders and stayed hidden, but when we got him out of there he was never the same. He became a bad alcoholic who drank every night till he passed out.

On another mission, the team got put in and then stayed on site and didn't move for three days. They had been set down right in the middle of an NVA battalion. The enemy was all around them, so close that an NVA soldier came up and almost urinated on one team member. But the whole team hid there for three days till the battalion moved. They couldn't eat or get up to use the bathroom, but they did not lose a single team member.

Staying hidden was part of the job and we got to be very good at finding ways to go undetected, too. For example, the NVA and VC often tracked us by looking for big American footprints, so SOG folks developed this overshoe that had a small footprint on the bottom that made it look like someone had walked through wearing the tire sandals the VC used.

I learned another trick from one of the prisoners I interrogated in an earlier tour. He told me, "You know we can smell you Americans?"

That's because we tended to eat a lot of red meat and dairy products, while the Vietnamese ate mostly fish. We just smelled different, so I stopped eating those American kinds of food when I was in SOG and began using the "armpit sauce" fish oil to lubricate my gun.

Like I said, most of what we were doing was recon, and we were doing a lot of that in the A Shau Valley and west into Laos. Our recon teams would find some interesting things, like a series of roads big enough to run a whole truck down at night, but the next day there would be trees there. What the NVA was doing was tying the tops of whole trees together and moving them out at night so the trucks could run, then moving them back in before daylight to cover the road.

One of the bad things was the rear-echelon folks didn't always believe what the recon people told them. One story was that supposedly a recon team reported the NVA was using elephants to move trees. Our higher headquarters people called the SOG men liars.

Well, a week later a recon team brought them a gift. A sack full of fresh elephant dung was left on someone's desk. They believed them after that. But the same thing happened with tanks. They'd say, "No, they are not utilizing tanks at all." The recon team would go in and take pictures of tanks and bring those pictures back, but they still didn't believe them. Finally the recon team went back in, used a little old rocket launcher, and brought them back part of the tank. They believed them from then on.

The higher-ups just couldn't realize the ingenuity of the NVA and how aware they were of us. For example, we had one team that was supposed to go in and try to find a pipeline they knew the NVA was using to get diesel fuel in for their trucks. The team found the pipeline and discovered that, at every three or four hundred feet of the pipeline, the NVA had installed a shutoff valve so if we blew the line they could shut it off on each side until the pipe was repaired.

Another problem we had was SOG did not have its own assets. It had to "borrow" them from other branches of the military, which caused a lot of confusion and frustration. One time we had a team in across the border maybe ten or twelve miles into Laos, and they got in trouble and asked for extraction. We sent in a full package of planes and men borrowed from another organization.

During the extraction the team took fire and before long we had three of the slicks down, the gunships were out of ammo, and the chase medic was on the ground. When the commander of that unit called and wanted to know where his aircraft were, we couldn't tell him. It was that top secret.

But the most difficult part of this was the internal people you had to work with, especially some of the South Vietnamese working for the other side. We were being infiltrated from every level, from the top down. For example, we had a SOG man who was shot down and captured and he spent time in a North Vietnamese prison camp. While he was there, he saw one of our SOG operators, a top-notch recon man who had run several SOG missions with us, come into camp. This man turned out to be a North Vietnamese captain who was reporting our missions back to the NVA.

This problem was so bad we got so we wouldn't tell the truth about where a team was, or where we were going to be, and actually lied to higher headquarters.

Another example of this kind of thing is how our personal information seemed to get out real easy. This became personal for me while I was in Phu Bai when someone brought me a copy of a big poster, probably eighteen by thirteen inches in size, that they had found. It was a "Wanted, Dead or Alive" poster with my picture on it. They had used a nice black-and-white photo of me from a Vietnamese driver's license I had been told to get on an earlier tour, but had never used.

I'm not sure why they wanted me, although it may have had something to do with the fact I had been decorated by the South Vietnamese government on my previous tours there, or maybe it was simply a sign I was doing my job well. It was definitely a sign that someone inside the South Vietnamese government who had access to our photos was supplying them to the enemy.

The reward was five hundred thousand piasters, which at the time would have been about one hundred thousand US dollars. All I could do was keep a low profile and hope no one turned me in.

I stayed at that SOG launch site for three months before Colonel Cole was moved down to SMAG, the Special Missions Advisory Group that was based in Nha Trang, and he took me with him. SMAG was designed to train the South Vietnamese high command to take over the command of SOG.

Now, Nha Trang, which was a sort of rest and recuperation center, should have been a super assignment, but to me it was just frustrating. That's because most of the South Vietnamese men we were training were not very good. I think that was because they had been selected to command this unit because of their political connections, not their military ability. And it may also have been that some of them who were officers did not like taking orders from a sergeant like me.

We did try to train them, though, and some of that training required giving these South Vietnamese commanders a little taste of what they would face on the ground. They didn't do too well at it. For example, we did some training on an island near Nha Trang where we were trying to teach them how to infiltrate from a rubber boat. We could get them in the boats, but we could not get them to maneuver or land them properly. They usually let the current take them, and a lot of times we would have to go get them out of the water.

We also tried similar training missions in the woods, but they weren't very good at those, either. All I knew was we were spending a tremendous amount of money to train them and they were not learning, so when I left there to come home about four months later, I knew things were not going to go well for the rest of the war.

CHAPTER TWENTY-ONE

LIFE GOES ON

WHEN I CAME BACK to the States from that third tour I faced some challenges. Now, I'll tell you I was glad to get some regular American food—our family didn't have too much rice for a while after I got back, though these days it's not so bad, especially if you put gravy on it. But there were other things to adjust to that were hard.

A big one was dealing with the attitudes of people in the States toward those of us who had served in Vietnam. Number one, it's hard to be called a "baby killer" when you didn't kill any babies, but it's even harder to hear that kind of thing when you were sent there by your own government, not by choice. I just learned to not tell people I had been in Vietnam.

Another challenge was that my orders when I came home from Vietnam were for me to go to Fort Huachuca, Arizona, which at the time was a US Army Communications Command (USACC). I went there as an operations sergeant, which is a staff NCO position at the battalion level or higher, but shortly after I got there they moved me to be a first sergeant, which to me was a demotion. Going from a combat arms position to a communications position was tough, too. I went from the top—an elite organization, the Special Forces—to what I thought of as the bottom.

At Fort Huachuca I was in charge of three sections. One was a group of the last draftees in the military who were all PhDs and PFCs and who didn't want to be there. All they wanted to do was get their two years in and get back to work. They were doing some highly classified work at this period of time, building guidance systems for missiles.

Another was a highly skilled group skilled in only one area. They were putting the leave and earning statements of the army into computers, which were much bigger and hard to use at that time than they are today, and had to be kept in conditions of constant temperature and pressure.

My third group was all of Secretary of Defense Robert S. McNamara's "Project 100,000." This was a program for recruits who could not pass the military's physical or written aptitude tests. The idea when it was started in 1966 was that the program could take in men who did not meet standard military mental or physical requirements and train them so they could make it in the military and later in the civilian world, and also to bring in more troops for the war effort. They started out with forty thousand men the first year and planned to bring in another one hundred thousand each year after that.

The program was also known as "McNamara's 100,000," but I called it "Project 100,000 Dumdums" because I couldn't do anything with them.

I was not happy there, but I got to leave after about two and a half years when I was fortunate enough to be picked up for class number three of the United States Army Sergeants Major Academy.

This was something new they had started in 1972 at Fort Bliss, Texas, and the first class had actually started in January 1973. We had instructors from the Command and General Staff College that were army sergeant majors who gave us an idea of what was going on.

When I finished at the academy, I was sent to Fort Bragg again where I was promoted to sergeant major and then sent to the Panama Canal Zone. There I was supposed to be a commandant of the NCO academy, but I had all of the NCO schools for that area and was also the command sergeant major for Fort Sherman on the Panama Canal.

I spent more than two years there and it was a great assignment, but it seemed like my children were loving it a little too much, so I decided I'd better get them back to the United States. I didn't like the assignment they were going to send me back to, though, which was some sort of administrative position, so in 1978 I decided it was time to retire from the military.

Now, Mary always thought we would stay in Fort Bragg when I retired, because that had been our home for so many years. But I didn't want to be where I could hear the bugles call reveille every morning, which I could from our house, and be where I might want to go on post all the time. I knew it was time for me to break from that life, and I wanted to finish my formal education. I had completed a lot of college correspondence credits and had also received two associate's degrees while I was in the military, but I wanted to get more formal education.

So we sold our house in North Carolina and moved back to Opelika, Alabama, where I had also bought a little farmland near Mary's family. I finished a bachelor's degree in business and accounting from Troy University, a degree I chose because I felt like it was something I could do for as long as I wanted to. I was about forty-four at the time and we had five kids, so I knew I would have to keep working for a long time.

Once I had that degree, I looked around for jobs, but it was hard for men who had served in Vietnam to find them. People still weren't over it, so I opened an accounting and tax consulting business in Auburn, Alabama, which is right next door to Opelika, and that was my primary focus for the next twenty-two years.

I also went on to get two master's degrees from Troy, one in foundations of education and another in management, then I did some master's work on a third degree in counseling and human development, but I elected not to finish that one. (I just needed ten hours to finish it, but the courses were not related to what I wanted to do.) In 2017, I got a third degree from Troy when they awarded me an honorary PhD. I guess that means I can now be called Dr. Adkins, in addition to Command Sergeant Major Adkins.

While my children were in college I needed some additional funds so, in addition to my accounting and tax business and also running some other small businesses and rental property in the area, I also worked as a college-level teacher. I taught adult education at Southern Union State Community College in Opelika for ten years, then I worked as an adjunct instructor for Auburn University teaching classes primarily in math and adult education.

When I was a kid back in Oklahoma, teaching was not something I thought I wanted to do, despite having gone to a teachers' college, but by the time I left the military it was a good fit for me. I was, after all, a teacher the entire time I was a Green Beret, so I think the decision to go into teaching after I retired was a by-product of that.

I did not suffer from posttraumatic stress disorder (PTSD). I found out the easy way for me to not dwell on what happened at A Shau or on my other tours in Vietnam was to focus on family and work. I stayed busy with our kids, my school, and work and working on my farm in Opelika. I guess the Oklahoma farm boy in me never went away. The bottom line is I didn't have time to think about it, and I did that intentionally.

I have had flashbacks, but anyone who has been in combat knows this might happen and we just deal with it. Some of us are capable of handling it much better than others. You learn how to balance that. But, yes, there are still things that trigger a reaction in me. For example, the sound of weapons will always be implanted in me because it's a survival strategy you learn the hard way in war. If I hear one of those automatic weapons now being sold as hunting rifles, to me it is still an enemy weapon.

I didn't keep up with any of the Vietnamese soldiers who fought with us at A Shau or anywhere else in Vietnam, and I don't know if any of them are still alive. I didn't really keep up with most of the Americans who fought with me in that terrible battle in A Shau Valley, either, though a few of us got together for a reunion at my house in 2003.

I have had a chance to reconnect with five of them, however, as we have written this book—Dave Blair, John Bradford, Victor Underwood, George Pointon, and Wayne Murray.

Like me, all five of these men did additional tours in Vietnam after A Shau, and they each went on to make a full military career before, also like me, they moved on to civilian life.

Dave Blair worked his way up to a full colonel in the army before he retired. He and his wife, Lavinia, settled in Tampa, Florida, where they tend to an interesting menagerie, including several different kinds of birds, a number of miniature horses, and dogs, and, as he says, "God knows how many cats."

Victor Underwood retired from the military as a master sergeant, and, always one for adventure and the great outdoors, helped sail a fishing boat from Jacksonville, Florida, back to Alaska, a trip that involved a Coast Guard rescue. After that he decided to stick to hunting and fishing and support Diane, who finally got to pursue her own career. They are now both fully retired and live in Chewelah, Washington, a small community outside Spokane where quail and deer wander through yards, and an occasional cougar is sighted in the neighborhood. "We're just kind of cooling our heels," he said. "We're all old farts now."

Wayne Murray did become a pilot, just like he swore he'd do after he almost accidentally blew up that pilot in A Shau, and served as an infantry branch aviator. He retired from the army as a major, then worked another thirty-one years as a civilian instructor pilot, training aviation branch officers at Fort Rucker. Before he passed away in July 2017, he lived out in the country near Daleville, Alabama, with his wife, Lisa, who is retired military herself.

John Bradford also became a pilot and retired as a major, then worked as the head of a security department for a Fortune 100 company for many years. He now lives with his wife, Janie, in Katy, Texas.

George Pointon, who still suffers from the "evil" pain of his A Shau wounds, stayed in the military for a number of years before becoming a defense industry consultant and running several small businesses in the United States and in Thailand, where he has lived for a number of years since.

I can't speak for these five men or any of the others who experienced the Battle of A Shau, but I can say I think we made a pretty good team there. If they wore that green beret, I knew they were quality people. It's like you're either pregnant or you're not. You're either a Special Forces soldier or you're not, and if you're a Special Forces soldier I know you've got my back.

The ones who have truly had my back all these years, though, are my supportive wife and family, quality people I always know I can rely on. Mary has been the strength of the family and, believe me, the family is super important for a military person.

CHAPTER TWENTY-TWO

A MATTER OF HONOR

FIGHTING IN THE BATTLE OF A SHAU certainly changed my life, but I did not want it to define my life. I think I have done a pretty good job of moving ahead since 1966, and I've been lucky to have a full and productive life for the past five decades. But little did I know that something a young captain who served with me at A Shau did in 1966 would, nearly fifty years later, change my life again.

That captain, Davis Blair, who was my commanding officer during A Shau, put my name up for the Medal of Honor not long after the battle occurred, but his recommendation didn't go anywhere.

There are a number of stories about why that happened. One is that the recommendation never got to the approving authorities.

Another is that General William Westmoreland, who commanded the US forces during the Vietnam War, or some other high member of his staff, stopped it. There's a rumor that one of them called the officer of the 5th Special Forces group at the time and said, "What are you doing, running a Medal of Honor factory?" because at that time period, all of the Medals of Honor awarded in Vietnam had gone to Special Forces.

Still another reason may be because of what happened with the shooting of the CIDG soldiers. Or it could have been because US Air Force Major Bernie Fisher, who had rescued "Jump" Myers from the airstrip during the battle, had been put forward as a medal candidate, and someone higher up didn't think it was appropriate to award a Medal of Honor to two men from the same battle.

At the time it did not matter to me, and I did receive the Distinguished Service Cross for the Battle of A Shau, which I wore proudly, as well as a long list of other awards for my service in Vietnam and in the military. Receiving the Medal of Honor was not something I expected or felt I needed, or even deserved, but Dave Blair, Victor Underwood, and others thought differently and did not stop trying.

One of my Special Forces captains, Jim Reed, who at one time had been my team leader back in the States, was living in Birmingham, Alabama, after he was discharged from the military. He had been involved in Special Forces operations in Cambodia and had been hit real hard. He worked on the recommendation for a long time, doing a lot of research and pulling it all together. About the time he was ready to submit it, though, he passed away, but his wife sent it to Colonel Blair who then got with Don Turner, an air force first sergeant who had become a minister, and they started working on it the second time.

I didn't realize it until years later, but Blair and Turner worked on it six and a half years. Turner had to go before a board of senior officers, which was a strictly secret board, and the board had to make a recommendation to the Department of the Army. From there it had to go to the secretary of the army, then to the secretary of defense, then to the House Armed Services Committee in Congress, then before the full House. It had to go through the same process in the Senate, too, and if one word changed on it, which did happen, it had to start all over again.

Once it made it through all those levels, the recommendation went to the president of the United States, who had the final authority to approve or disapprove the recommendation.

But it was even more complicated for me, because federal law at the time stated the Medal of Honor had to be awarded within three years of the action. By this time, it had been almost fifty years since the Battle of A Shau, so before they could award it to me, they had to change the law or make an exception for my case. The bill that came through Congress to make that change kept getting hijacked by other political dealings, so it was quite a process, but it finally passed. My congressman, Mike Rogers, was co-sponsor of the bill and he pushed it through. Without him I would never have had the opportunity to wear this medal.

I received a phone call in early June 2014 from someone at the Pentagon who said I should expect a phone call on June 11 at a certain time from a high-ranking government official.

I anticipated it was someone who was working the MIA and POW recoveries from that era.

The time came and the wife and I were both on the call and it was the president of the United States, Barack Obama, on the phone. He said, "I have approved the Medal of Honor for you based upon the recommendation of the secretary of defense."

He congratulated me and said someone would be in touch soon about plans for the medal ceremony.

They placed a gag order on me and said an announcement about the medal was not to be released to the news media until it was released by the White House first. Then the Pentagon got in touch with me the same day and started setting things up.

Over the next few weeks we were busy. A Pentagon official came to my home in Opelika just a few days after that phone call and started briefing me on how this would work. We communicated with someone almost daily as we got ready for the ceremony, and they took me over to Fort Benning to get fitted for a new uniform and also get training to learn how to handle the media once we got to DC.

A few days before the medal ceremony, a limousine came and got me and Mary and took us to the Atlanta airport, where they moved us through with an official beside us the whole way. From that time on, we were watched constantly.

They sent me over to the Pentagon for one last fitting of my uniform; they wanted to make sure it was perfect. They put a lieutenant with me, and she did a great job assisting us throughout the medal proceedings and the next several days of events. Anywhere we went in the DC area we had a blue-light escort.

On the morning of September 15, 2014, the Pentagon police came in a motorcycle convoy and took me and my immediate family to the White House. We were called into the Oval Office where President Obama signed the order in front of us. Photos were taken and then we had the official ceremony, a full ceremony with all the military and civilian dignitaries present to include several of the other living Medal of Honor recipients, and almost one hundred friends and family members. I was honored to have all those people attend the ceremony. I was humbled that John Bradford, Victor Underwood, Davis Blair, and Wayne Murray came.

The president awarded me the medal, officially hanging it around my neck on a stage in the White House, and then there was a reception. Everyone told me the food at the reception was great, but I didn't get to eat much of it. We then had a press conference and another blue-light escort back to the hotel.

The next day, we were in the Pentagon with the secretary of defense, who hosted the program there for us as I was inducted into the Pentagon's Hall of Heroes, including a small luncheon with the under secretary and the sergeant major of the army and my immediate family. That food was quite good and I did get to eat it. After lunch we went to the auditorium for the ceremony, and at this time they gave me an official citation and the Medal of Honor flag.

After that, we spent the next several days and nights attending receptions with the sergeant major of the army, the

Special Forces Association, and the secretary of defense and touring the capital and Congress.

When I returned back home to Opelika, two or three things were really hard to handle because they were so humbling. The Lee County sheriff, Jay Jones, brought me a flag that flew over the Lee County Justice Center the day of my ceremony. Opelika mayor Gary Fuller presented me with the flag that flew over Opelika the day I received the Medal of Honor. My grandson Blake Adkins, who had interned with Congressman Mike Rogers that summer, brought me the flag that flew over the US Capitol Building the day of my Medal of Honor ceremony. I now have a lot of flags, but I am grateful to have them all.

Since that time, my life has changed drastically. I have traveled all over the United States for all kinds of events including the wreath-laying at President Kennedy's grave in Arlington National Cemetery, and the New York Stock Exchange in lower Manhattan, where I missed ringing the closing bell the first time I was there because I was talking to someone, but on other trips back since then I have had that honor.

I've also been able to do a lot with Special Forces, including speaking at the graduation for a Special Forces class at Fort Bragg and getting to see a HALO demonstration at Yuma, Arizona. One of the instructors got out of an airplane at about twenty-five thousand feet, fell for about a minute and a half, popped his chute at about five thousand feet, then opened a flag in my honor and came down as it flew beside him. He brought it to me once he was on the ground. I guess I could have tried that jump myself and had one more "commute" to work, but Mary vetoed me jumping.

I'd have a hard time listing all the places I've been now and all the organizations that have honored me by asking me to attend meetings and speak. Those range from our local churches and civic groups to national veterans' associations.

I was particularly honored to be on hand when Gainesville, Texas, dedicated a beautiful monument to veterans and planted a tree there in my honor. And one of my greatest honors has been that my hometown, Waurika, Oklahoma, commissioned a sculpture of me that is in a veteran's park there. Several people I went to school with came to that event. My niece Amber Hayes, who is a singer and songwriter in Nashville, also wrote a song in my honor, "Hero's Heart."

Everywhere I go I am treated very well. The rule is that Medal of Honor recipients rank higher in official protocol than a sitting member of Congress, and frequently an armed guard is following me because of concerns I might be a target for some sort of terrorist act. But I'll tell you, I do not intend to be taken prisoner.

At this stage in my life it is an exhausting schedule, but I believe this is my role. We're down to just seventy-two living Medal of Honor recipients representing about thirty million Americans who have served this country. A number of those living medal recipients are no longer able to travel, so I will go to represent them whenever I can and for as long as I can.

To wear the medal on my neck is super humbling, especially when people recognize it or stop and ask me about it, because it gives me a chance to explain why I wear it. Since the day the medal was placed around my neck, I've made it known I wear it not for myself, but for the other sixteen American Special Forces soldiers who were at A Shau with me.

I am not a hero. They are the real heroes. All sixteen were decorated for valor and all sixteen were wounded, most of them multiple times, and unfortunately five of those soldiers paid the ultimate price of giving their lives for the cause. They are the heroes and I am only their representative at this time.

CHAPTER TWENTY-THREE

REGRETS AND LESSONS

I've NOT BEEN BACK to Vietnam since I left there at the end of my last tour in 1971. I don't want to go back. There's nothing there I want to revisit and it's possible, after all, that there is still a price on my head.

But that does not mean I can't look back, and when I do look back I see both regrets and lessons learned, or worth learning.

One of my greatest regrets is that we left behind men, particularly Jimmy Taylor. I know we did everything we could to find him, and I know Jimmy's family members have been very understanding. Several years ago, Jimmy's brother told John Bradford, "You couldn't take a body with you when you're being chased by the bad guys."

That regret will never go away, but the hope that we may someday find Jimmy Taylor doesn't go away, either. At the present time, more than one thousand Americans are still listed as missing in action in Vietnam, Laos, and Cambodia, but our government and other groups are working hard to recover those men. And they have had some success at that. A few years ago, for example, they found the body of a Special Forces soldier who was killed in another camp overrun after A Shau. His body was brought back home and his former commanding officer in Vietnam, who had become a preacher, was there to perform his burial service.

That gives me hope that we may someday find them all, including Jimmy Taylor.

I also regret that we left behind our allies in Vietnam, the Montagnard people. They gave their all for us, and I wish we Green Berets had been able to thank them by fulfilling our motto and freeing them from oppression. We did not, and even though some two thousand Montagnards were brought to the United States in the mid-1970s and have established thriving communities here, I regret we didn't help more of them. I do know, however, that they are a strong people with a strong culture that I hope will survive for generations to come.

Me giving George Pointon a blood expander in his leg is not something I regret, but I understand there are a lot of Special Forces soldiers who do. That technique is now part of their training, and when they end up with sore places on their legs from practicing that procedure they have me to thank. Their "thanks" is understandably not always given in real nice language, though.

There are other things that happened during the Vietnam War I think have or can offer us a chance to learn lessons for today and the future.

One lesson I believe we did learn is the importance of teaching our troops, especially our Special Forces people, about language and culture. I made a few mistakes in those areas when I was in Vietnam, and I had some difficulties because I did not know enough about the customs and languages of the Vietnamese people.

I'm happy to say, though, that Special Forces training now requires Green Berets to be proficient in the languages of the countries where they serve. To do this, they offer intensive foreign language and culture classes at all Special Forces training centers. Though we did some language training when I was in Special Forces, it was not enough to really help us communicate with the people in those countries.

And I think Special Forces and other branches of the military continue to do something we did so well in Vietnam and other places: build relationships in the communities where we were serving by providing health and engineering assistance in those communities.

I do have some concerns about the lessons we may or may not have learned, though. One of the problems we faced in Vietnam, and throughout my military career, was that soldiers were often kept downrange too long, especially our SOG men. I don't think we have learned a lesson about that yet because it still happens today. But I think that has to do with another lesson we need to learn—we need to do a better job of supporting our military.

At this time, less than one percent of our population serves in the military. That means less than one percent of us are helping protect our way of life. That one percent is probably the best-trained and the best-educated military we have ever had, but I am not sure one percent is enough to take care of multiple military engagements like we have today in the Middle East,

Africa, the Philippines, Korea, and South America. We need to do something about that, and I think that "something" is to make sure our leaders provide sufficient funding for our military.

It also means we must make staying in the military more attractive to those who are currently serving, which may be a lesson we have learned. I understand they offer some nice reenlistment bonuses to highly trained, fully qualified Special Forces soldiers these days. They didn't have that in my time, and unfortunately they won't let me reenlist now.

I am also not sure we have learned much about getting into a conflict with no clear goal. When I went over to Vietnam, I didn't really know what the politics were, but that's because they changed. For example, when I first went over there I was not allowed to fire a weapon unless I was fired at. That rapidly changed as we became combatants, not advisors, but then the United States decided to withdraw and our roles went back to being advisors again. The politics and policies kept changing.

I understand the problem we had in Vietnam with the enemy infiltrating our camps still goes on today, especially in the Middle East and Africa. Maybe indigenous people don't set out to do this. Their loyalty is to their own survival and they may have to switch sides. If there's a lesson to be learned there it is that we have to be diligent in maintaining security for our troops and facilities.

There are other lessons we can and should learn from Vietnam, and I hope we can look back and do that still. But for me, the big personal lesson is this: don't go back.

COMMAND SERGEANT MAJOR BENNIE GENE ADKINS

PRESENTED SEPT. 15, 2014

Sergeant First Class Bennie G. Adkins distinguished himself by acts of gallantry and intrepidity at the risk of his life above and beyond the call of duty while serving as an Intelligence Sergeant with Detachment A-102, 5th Special Forces Group, 1st Special Forces, during combat operations against an armed enemy at Camp A Shau, Republic of Vietnam from March 9 to 12, 1966. When the camp was attacked by a large North Vietnamese and Viet Cong force in the early morning hours, Sergeant First Class Adkins rushed through intense enemy fire and manned a mortar position continually adjusting fire for the camp, despite incurring wounds as the mortar pit received several direct hits from enemy mortars. Upon learning that several soldiers were wounded near the center of camp, he temporarily turned the mortar over to another soldier, ran through exploding mortar rounds and dragged several comrades to safety. As the hostile fire subsided, Sergeant First Class Adkins exposed himself to sporadic sniper fire while carrying his wounded comrades to the camp dispensary. When Sergeant First Class Adkins and his group of defenders came under heavy small arms fire from members of the Civilian Irregular Defense Group that had defected to fight with the North Vietnamese, he maneuvered outside the camp to evacuate a seriously wounded American and draw fire all the while successfully covering the rescue. When a resupply airdrop landed outside of the camp perimeter, Sergeant First Class Adkins, again, moved outside of the camp walls to retrieve the much-needed supplies. During the early morning hours of March 10, 1966 enemy forces launched their main attack and within two hours, Sergeant First Class Adkins was the only man firing a mortar weapon. When all mortar rounds were expended, Sergeant First Class Adkins began placing effective recoilless rifle fire upon enemy positions. Despite receiving additional wounds from enemy rounds exploding on his position, Sergeant First Class Adkins fought off intense waves of attacking Viet Cong. Sergeant First Class Adkins eliminated numerous insurgents with small arms fire after withdrawing to a communications bunker with several soldiers. Running extremely low on ammunition, he returned to the mortar pit, gathered vital ammunition and ran through intense fire back to the bunker. After being ordered to evacuate the camp, Sergeant First Class Adkins and a small group of soldiers destroyed all signal equipment and classified documents, dug their way out of the rear of the bunker and fought their way out of the camp. While carrying a wounded soldier to the extraction point he learned that the last helicopter had already departed. Sergeant First Class Adkins led the group while evading the enemy until they were rescued by helicopter on March 12, 1966. During the thirty-eight-hour battle and forty-eight hours of escape and evasion, fighting with mortars, machine guns, recoilless rifles, small arms, and hand grenades, it was estimated that Sergeant First Class Adkins killed between one hundred thirty-five and one hundred seventy-five of the enemy while sustaining eighteen different wounds to his body. Sergeant First Class Adkins' extraordinary heroism and selflessness above and beyond the call of duty are in keeping with the highest traditions of the military service and reflect great credit upon himself, Detachment A-102, 5th Special Forces Group, 1st Special Forces and the United States Army.

OTHER DECORATIONS ENTITLED TO
COMMAND SERGEANT MAJOR BENNIE G. ADKINS

- Distinguished Service Cross
- Silver Star
- Bronze Star Medal with one Bronze Oak Leaf Cluster and "V" Device
- Purple Heart with two Bronze Oak Leaf Clusters
- Army Commendation Medal
- Army Good Conduct Medal with Bronze Clasp and Five Loops
- National Defense Service Medal
- Armed Forces Expeditionary Medal
- Vietnam Service Medal with one Silver Service Star and one Bronze Service Star
- Presidential Unit Citation
- Meritorious Unit Citation

- Republic of Vietnam Campaign Medal with "60" Device
- Republic of Vietnam Bravery Medal with Brass Star
- Republic of Vietnam Gallantry Cross with Bronze Star
- Republic of Vietnam Gallantry Cross Unit Citation with Palm Device
- Combat Infantryman Badge
- Special Forces Tab
- US Army Master Parachutist Badge
- Vietnamese Parachutist Badge (two awards)
- Expert Badge with Rifle and Pistol Bars
- Sharpshooter Badge with Carbine Bar
- Marksman Badge with Machinegun Bar

ACKNOWLEDGMENTS

As my co-author and I started this book project, we made every effort we could to locate any and all surviving A Shau veterans. We were lucky enough to find five of them, without whom this book would not have been possible.

Chief among that group is Davis Blair, whose extensive collection of memories, records, and photographs related to the battle were pivotal to getting our facts right. We are eternally grateful for Blair's many contributions to this project. The memories shared by Victor and Diane Underwood, who also allowed us to use their collection of photos and correspondences, and of Wayne Murray, John Bradford, and George Pointon were equally invaluable and helped bring this story to life.

I also owe a huge debt of gratitude to Blair and others who kept working on my Medal of Honor nomination for all those years since 1966, and also to Alabama Congressman Mike Rogers who helped shepherd the legislation through Congress that allowed the MOH to be bestowed upon me 48 years after the battle.

In addition, my co-author and I thank Johnny Lawrence, a mutual friend who introduced us to one another and helped make this writing partnership happen. We are appreciative for the help of our agent, Doug Grad, who found the perfect home for this book, and we are deeply grateful to Bob Pigeon at Da

Capo Press, who believed in this story and in us and patiently, generously helped us through this process. Many thanks, too, to Christine Marra, the editor who made this book shine, and to the many others at Da Capo who supported us as this book took shape. And a very special thank you to Chuck Hagel for not only writing the Foreword for this book, but also writing the letter of recommendation that led to my receiving the MOH on September 15, 2014.

Finally, there are two groups of people that deserve the greatest thanks of all. The first group includes the sixteen men who fought so valiantly with me at A Shau, five of whom paid the ultimate price, and their families. They, along with the many other service men and women—past, present, and future—who have protected our country in times of conflict and continue to do so today, deserve so much more than a thank you—they deserve our undying respect.

The other group includes our family members, who have supported us throughout this project and in so many other ways in life. I am deeply and continually grateful for the support of my children, Michael and Keith Adkins and Mary Ann Adkins Blake, and I most especially thank my wife, Mary, who has been there every step of the way and never stopped supporting me through my years in the military and beyond. My co-author also thanks her entire family for their support, especially her husband, Kevin, who served not only as an outside reader for us, but who kept the home fires burning during the long hours of research and writing required to create this book.

We are honored to tell this story and honored to have had so much help in writing—and living—this story.

—*Bennie G. Adkins and Katie Lamar Jackson*

INDEX